ROOMS
FOR RENT
IN THE
OUTER
PLANETS

ROOMS FOR RENT IN THE OUTER PLANETS

*Selected Poems
1962 – 1996*

AL PURDY

*Selected and
edited by*
AL PURDY
and
SAM SOLECKI

**HARBOUR
PUBLISHING**

Harbour Publishing
Box 219
Madeira Park, BC V0N 2H0

Cover art: Vincent Van Gogh, *Café terrace at night, "Place du Forum," Arles,* collection Kröller-Müller Museum, Otterlo, The Netherlands. Cover design by Roger Handling, Terra Firma. Page design & layout by David Lee Communications.

Published with the assistance of the Canada Council and the Government of British Columbia, Cultural Services Branch. Printed and bound in Canada.

The poems from *Piling Blood* and *Naked with Summer in Your Mouth* are reprinted by permission of McClelland and Stewart. With the exception of "Spring Song", "Voltaire" and "Elegy for a Grandfather," the poems that appeared in *The Collected Poems of Al Purdy* (1986) are reprinted in the versions published in that volume. The excerpts in the "Afterword" were chosen by Sam Solecki, who also edited the volume for the press.

Canadian Cataloguing in Publication Data

Purdy, Al, 1918–
  Rooms for rent in the outer planets

  ISBN 1-55017-148-8

  I. Title.
PS8531.U8A6 1996   C811'.54   C96-910487-1
PR9199.3.P8A6 1996

CONTENTS

For Eurithe

O what am I, that I should not seem
For the song's sake a fool?

W.B. Yeats
"A Prayer for Old Age"

THE DEAD POET

I was altered in the placenta
by the dead brother before me
who built a place in the womb
knowing I was coming:
he wrote words on the walls of flesh
painting a woman inside a woman
whispering a faint lullaby
that sings in my blind heart still

The others were lumberjacks
backwoods wrestlers and farmers
their women were meek and mild
nothing of them survives
but an image inside an image
of a cookstove and the kettle boiling
— how else explain myself to myself
where does the song come from?

Now on my wanderings:
at the Alhambra's lyric dazzle
where the Moors built stone poems
a wan white face peering out
— and the shadow in Plato's cave
remembers the small dead one
— at Samarkand in pale blue light
the words came slowly from him
— I recall the music of blood
on the Street of the Silversmiths

Sleep softly spirit of earth
as the days and nights join hands
when everything becomes one thing
wait softly brother
but do not expect it to happen

that great whoop announcing resurrection
expect only a small whisper
of birds nesting and green things growing
and a brief saying of them
and know where the words came from

SPRING SONG

— philosophic musings from under an
old Pontiac while changing the oil and
observing a young lady in summer attire
on her way to the rural mail box —

You neanderthals with guns and bombs
stop exactly where you are
assassins wait in your own dark thoughts
and armies marching thru the rain
with rifles dragging in the mud halt
with one foot raised to take a step
teetering at the dark crossroads
consulting your maps of hell
stop exactly where you are

The world's pain is a little away from here
and the hawk's burst of speed that claws
a fish from its glass house is earlier
and later than now under a rejuvenated
Pontiac with frogs booming temporary
sonatas for mortals and Beethoven
crows thronging the June skies and
everything still
                everything suddenly goddam still
the sun a hovering golden bird
                nothing moves

soft clouds wait
like floating houses in the sky
and the storm beyond the horizon waits
planets stopped in their tracks
high over the village of Ameliasburg
      as if forever was now
      and the grass roots knew it all
— but they don't you know and here I am
      with both hands high
under the skirts of the world
trying to figure it out too late for
someone breathed or sighed or spoke
and everything rearranged itself
from is to was the white moon tracks
her silver self across the purple night
replacing time with a celestial
hour glass halfway between a girl
and woman I forgot till she comes jiggling
back from the dark mailbox at last migawd
hosanna in the lowest mons veneris I
will never get to change the goddam oil

REMAINS OF AN INDIAN VILLAGE

Underfoot rotten boards, forest rubble, bones . . .
Animals were here after the plague,
after smallpox to make another ending:
for the tutelary gods of decay
acknowledge aid from any quarter . . .
Here the charging cotyledons of spring
press green forefingers
on femurs, vertebrae, and delicate
belled skulls of children;
the moon's waylaid light does not shrink

13

from bone relics and other beauties of nature . . .

Death is certainly absent now,
at least in the overwhelming sense
that it once walked at night in the village
and howled thru the mouths of dogs —
But everything fades
and wavers into something else,
the seasonal cycle and the planet's rhythm
vary imperceptibly into the other;
spirits of the dead are vanished,
only great trees remain,
and the birth certificate of cedars
specifies no memory of a village . . .

(And I have seen myself fade
from a woman's eyes
while I was standing there,
and the earth was aware of
me no longer —)
But I come here as part of the process
in the pale morning light,
thinking what has been thought by no one
for years of their absence,
in some way continuing them —
And I observe the children's shadows
running in this green light from
                              a distant star
into the near forest —
wood violets and trilliums of
a hundred years ago
blooming and vanishing —
the villages of the brown people
toppling and returning —
What moves and lives
        occupying the same space,

what touches what touched them

                              owes them . . .

Standing knee-deep in the joined earth
of their weightless bones,
in the archaeological sunlight,
the trembling voltage of summer,
in the sunken reservoirs of rain,
standing waist-deep in the criss-cross
rivers of shadows,
in the village of nightfall,
the hunters silent and women
bending over dark fires,
I hear their broken consonants . . .

AT THE QUINTE HOTEL

I am drinking
I am drinking beer with yellow flowers
in underground sunlight
and you can see that I am a sensitive man
And I notice that the bartender is a sensitive man too
so I tell him about his beer
I tell him the beer he draws
is half fart and half horse piss
and all wonderful yellow flowers
But the bartender is not quite
so sensitive as I supposed he was
the way he looks at me now
and does not appreciate my exquisite analogy
Over in one corner two guys
are quietly making love
in the brief prelude to infinity
Opposite them a peculiar fight

15

enables the drinkers to lay aside
their comic books and watch with interest
as I watch with interest
A wiry little man slugs another guy
then tracks him bleeding into the toilet
and slugs him to the floor again
with ugly red flowers on the tile
three minutes later he roosters over
to the table where his drunk friend sits
with another friend and slugs both
of em ass-over-electric-kettle
so I have to walk around
on my way for a piss
Now I am a sensitive man
so I say to him mildly as hell
"You shouldn'ta knocked over that good beer
with them beautiful flowers in it"
So he says to me "Come on"
So I Come On
like a rabbit with weak kidneys I guess
like a yellow streak charging
on flower power I suppose
& knock the shit outa him & sit on him
(he is just a little guy)
and say reprovingly
"Violence will get you nowhere this time chum
Now you take me
I am a sensitive man
and would you believe I write poems?"
But I could see the doubt in his upside down face
in fact in all the faces
"What kinda poems?"
"Flower poems"
"So tell us a poem"
I got off the little guy but reluctantly
for he was comfortable

and told them this poem
They crowded around me with tears
in their eyes and wrung my hands feelingly
for my pockets for
it was a heart-warming moment for Literature
and moved by the demonstrable effect
of great Art and the brotherhood of people I remarked
"— the poem oughta be worth some beer"
It was a mistake of terminology
for silence came
and it was brought home to me in the tavern
that poems will not really buy beer or flowers
or a goddam thing
and I was sad
for I am a sensitive man

HOUSE GUEST

For two months we quarrelled over socialism   poetry   how to boil
    water
doing the dishes   carpentry   Russian steel production figures and
    whether
you could believe them and whether Toronto Leafs would take it all
that year and maybe hockey was rather like a good jazz combo
never knowing what came next
Listening
how the new house built with salvaged old lumber
bent a little in the wind and dreamt of the trees it came from
the time it was travelling thru
and the world of snow moving all night in its blowing sleep
while we discussed ultimate responsibility for a pile of dirty dishes
Jews in the Negev   the Bible as mythic literature   Peking Man
and in early morning looking outside to see the pink shapes of wind

printed on snow and a red sun tumbling upward almost touching the
    house
and fretwork tracks of rabbits outside where the window light
    had lain
last night an audience
watching in wonderment the odd human argument
that uses words instead of teeth
and got bored and went away

Of course there was wild grape wine and a stove full of Douglas fir
(railway salvage) and lake ice cracking its knuckles in hard Ontario
    weather
and working with saw and hammer at the house all winter afternoon
disagreeing about how to pound nails
arguing vehemently over how to make good coffee
Marcus Aurelius   Spartacus   Plato and François Villon
And it used to frustrate him terribly
that even when I was wrong he couldn't prove it
and when I agreed with him he was always suspicious
and thought he must be wrong because I said he was right
Every night the house shook from his snoring
a great motor driving us on into daylight
and the vibration was terrible
Every morning I'd get up and say "Look at the nails —
you snored them out half an inch in the night — "
He'd believe me at first and look and get mad and glare
and stare angrily out the window while I watched 10 minutes of
    irritation
drain from his eyes onto fields and farms and miles and miles of snow
We quarrelled over how dour I was in early morning
and how cheerful he was for counterpoint
and I argued that a million years of evolution
from snarling apeman have to be traversed before noon
and the desirability of murder in a case like his
and whether the Etruscans were really Semites
the Celtic invasion of Britain   European languages   Roman law

we argued about white being white (prove it dammit)   &
    cockroaches
bedbugs in Montreal   separatism   Nietzsche   Iroquois
    horsebreakers on the prairie
death of the individual and the ultimate destiny of man
and one night we quarrelled over how to cook eggs
In the morning driving to town we hardly spoke
and water poured downhill outside all day for it was spring
when we were gone with frogs mentioning lyrically
Russian steel production figures on Roblin Lake which were almost nil
I left him hitch-hiking on #2 Highway to Montreal
and I guess I was wrong about those eggs

THE CARIBOO HORSES

At 100 Mile House the cowboys ride in rolling
stagey cigarettes with one hand reining
half-tame bronco rebels on a morning grey as stone
— so much like riding dangerous women
     with whiskey coloured eyes —
such women as once fell dead with their lovers
with fire in their heads and slippery froth on thighs
— Beaver or Carrier women maybe or
     Blackfoot squaws far past the edge of this valley
on the other side of those two toy mountain ranges
     from the sunfierce plains beyond

But only horses
     waiting in stables
hitched at taverns
     standing at dawn
pastured outside the town with
jeeps and fords and chevys and
busy muttering stake trucks rushing

importantly over roads of man's devising
over the safe known roads of the ranchers
families and merchants of the town
                    On the high prairie
are only horse and rider
                    wind in dry grass
clopping in silence under the toy mountains
dropping sometimes and
                    lost in the dry grass
                    golden oranges of dung

Only horses
                    no stopwatch memories or palace ancestors
not Kiangs hauling undressed stone in the Nile Valley
and having stubborn Egyptian tantrums or
Onagers racing thru Hither Asia and
the last Quagga screaming in African highlands
                    lost relatives of these
                    whose hooves were thunder
the ghosts of horses battering thru the wind
whose names were the wind's common usage
whose life was the sun's
                    arriving here at chilly noon
                    in the gasoline smell of the
                    dust and waiting 15 minutes
                    at the grocer's

~~~

Song of the Impermanent Husband

Oh I would
I would in a minute
if the cusswords and bitter anger couldn't —
if the either/or quarrel didn't —
and the fat around my middle wasn't —

if I was young if
                    I wasn't so damn sure
I couldn't find another maddening bitch
like you holding on for dear life to
all the different parts of me for
twenty or twenty
                    thousand years
I'd leave in the night like
a disgraced caviar salesman
                    descend the moonlight
stairs to Halifax
                    (uh — no — not Halifax)
well then Toronto
                    ah
I guess not Toronto either/or
rain-soaked Vancouver down
                              down
                                   down
the dark stairs to
the South Seas' sunlit milky reefs and
          the jungle's green
                    unending bank account with
all the brown girls being brown
                    as they can be and all
the one-piece behinds stretched tight tonight
in small sarongs gawd not to be touched tho Oh
beautiful as an angel's ass
— without the genitals
And me
          in Paris like a smudged Canadian postcard and
(dear me)
          all the importuning white and lily girls
of rue Pigalle
                    and stroll
the sodden London streets and
                    find a sullen foggy woman who

enjoyed my odd colonial ways and send
a postcard back to you about my faithfulness and
talk about the lovely beastly English weather
I'd be the slimiest most uxorious wife deserter
                my shrunk amoeba self absurd inside
a saffron girl's geography and
hating me between magnetic nipples
but
    fooling no one
in all the sad and much emancipated world
Why then I'll stay
              at least for tea for
all the brownness is too brown and
all the whiteness too damned white
and I'm afraid
          afraid of being
any other woman's man
who might be me
         afraid
the unctuous and uneasy self I glimpse
sometimes might lose my faint and yapping cry
for being anything
              was never quite what I intended
And you you
        bitch no irritating
questions re love and permanence only
         an unrolling lifetime here
between your rocking thighs

       and the semblance of motion

NECROPSY OF LOVE

If it came about you died
it might be said I loved you:
love is an absolute as death is,
and neither bears false witness to the other —
But you remain alive.

No, I do not love you
                    hate the word,
that private tyranny inside a public sound,
your freedom's yours and not my own:
but hold my separate madness like a sword,
and plunge it in your body all night long.

If death shall strip our bones of all but bones,
then here's the flesh and flesh that's drunken-sweet
as wine cups in deceptive lunar light:
reach up your hand and turn the moonlight off,
and maybe it was never there at all,
so never promise anything to me:
but reach across the darkness with your hand,
reach across the distance of tonight,
and touch the moving moment once again
                    before you fall asleep —

HOCKEY PLAYERS

What they worry about most is injuries
                    broken arms and legs and
fractured skulls opening so doctors
can see such bloody beautiful things almost
not quite happening in the bone rooms
                    as they happen outside

And the referee?
        He's right there on the ice
not out of sight among the roaring blue gods
of a game played for passionate stockbrokers
children wearing business suits
and a nation of television agnostics
who never agree with the referee and applaud
when he falls flat on his face

        On a breakaway
the centreman carrying the puck
his wings trailing a little
           on both sides why
I've seen the aching glory of a resurrection
        in their eyes
         if they score
but crucifixion's agony to lose
— the game?

        We sit up there in the blues
bored and sleepy and suddenly three men
break down the ice in roaring feverish speed and
we stand up in our seats with such a rapid pouring
of delight exploding out of self to join them why
theirs and our orgasm is the rocket stipend
for skating thru the smoky end boards out
of sight and climbing up the appalachian highlands
and racing breast to breast across laurentian barrens
over hudson's diamond bay and down the treeless tundra where
auroras are tubercular and awesome and
stopping isn't feasible or possible or lawful
but we have to and we have to
                laugh because we must and
stop to look at self and one another but
        our opponent's never geography
           or distance why

it's men
— just men?

And how do the players feel about it
this combination of ballet and murder?
For years a Canadian specific
to salve the anguish of inferiority
by being good at something the Americans aren't
And what's the essence of a game like this
which takes a ten-year fragment of a man's life
replaced with love that lodges in his brain
                and substitutes for reason?
Besides the fear of injuries
is it the difficulty of ever really overtaking
a hard black rubber disc?
— Boys playing a boy's game in a permanent childhood
with a screaming coach who insists on winning
sports-writer-critics and the crowd gone mad?
— And the worrying wives wanting you to quit and
your aching body stretched on the rubbing table
thinking of money in owner's pockets that might be yours
the butt-slapping camaraderie and the self-indulgence
of allowing yourself to be a hero and knowing
everything ends in a pot-belly

Out on the ice can all these things be forgotten
in swift and skilled delight of speed?
— roaring out the endboards out the city
streets and high up where laconic winds
whisper litanies for a fevered hockey player
Or racing breast to breast and never stopping
over rooftops of the world and all together
sing the song of winning all together
sing the song of money all together

(and out in the suburbs
there's the six-year-old kid
whose reflexes were all wrong
who always fell down and hurt himself and cried
and never learned to skate
                with his friends)

HOME-MADE BEER

I was justly annoyed 10 years ago
in Vancouver: making beer in a crock
under the kitchen table when this
next-door youngster playing with my own
kid managed to sit down in it and
emerged with one end malted —
With excessive moderation I yodelled
at him
            "Keep your ass out of my beer!"
        and the little monster fled —
Whereupon my wife appeared from the bathroom
where she had been brooding for days
over the injustice of being a woman and
attacked me with a broom —
With commendable savoir faire I broke
the broom across my knee (it hurt too) and
then she grabbed the breadknife and made
for me with fairly obvious intentions —
I tore open my shirt and told her calmly
with bared breast and a minimum of boredom
        "Go ahead! Strike! Go ahead!"
Icicles dropped from her fiery eyes as she
snarled
            "I wouldn't want to go to jail

for killing a thing like you!"
I could see at once that she loved me
tho it was cleverly concealed —
For the next few weeks I had to distribute
the meals she prepared among neighbouring
dogs because of the rat poison and
addressed her as Missus Borgia —
That was a long time ago and while
at the time I deplored her lack of
self-control I find myself sentimental
about it now for it can never happen again —

Sept. 22, 1964: PS, I was wrong —

ONE RURAL WINTER

Trapped
      abandoned
            marooned
like a city thief in a country jail
bitching about all the fresh air
the rural mail my only communication with outside
surrounded by nothing
          but beautiful trees
          and I hate beautiful trees
I'm lost beyond even the remote boundaries
of Ameliasburg
        and I ask you
what could be more remote than a burg
named after a German dumpling named Amelia?
Why just close your eyes tight shut here
and you don't see little dots of light
         — you see fresh cowpads
But it's winter now

                    beyond the economic wall
(I have two nickels a dime and quarter
and not a damn cent
in my pockets but a wife
who comes out at night when I'm asleep
and won't meet the burning stare
of my closed dreaming womanless eyes
not for two nickels a dime and quarter anyway)

                    In the backyard
phallic pieces of wood and stones embedded
in ice (notice the Freudian terminology please)
a failed writer I'm trapped forever
in the 3rd Post-Atomic Pre-Literate Glacial Period
(making witty remarks like "Cold out, ain't it Zeke?")
It's got so I'm even afraid to go outside
in order to experience the rich rural experience
that is part of our common Canadian heritage
I might catch my foot in a lateral moraine or something
and be trapped forever
                    in Ameliasburg Township

The earth is frozen
the beautiful trees are frozen
even the mailbox's metal nose is cold
and I'm getting a little chilly myself
living in a house I built one tropical summer
with Unemployment Insurance money
                    and a bad-tempered wife
But I got into this mess myself
and I ain't blamin the Class Struggle
besides things are gonna get better
in ten or twenty years I think

It does improve my character
                    no doubt of that

to walk half a mile to the outdoor shithouse
with the temperature at 40 below
But *Maclean's* magazine is absorbing toilet tissue
and all the spiders and microbes and things
I trained last summer to sit up and chant
in unison Hallelujah What a Bum
                    to visiting imaginary females
from the neighbouring seminary
                — are frozen stiff
But the place is warm and comfortable
despite the perfumed gale below
as long as you can keep your mind
                  on the beautiful girl
tacked on the wall who advises that
            SPRING IS HERE
and I should have my crankcase flushed out
Then wiped and buttoned and zippered
I plunge back to the house
thru a white world of nothing
            but snow
                and the damn WIND
steals all my internal heat
it howls like a dog in my summer underwear
my heavy body is doped with wind and cold
            and the house door
            drags me into the hall
            and the door knob
            is a handle
I hold onto the sky with

Winter at Roblin Lake

Seeing the sky darken & the fields
turn brown & the lake lead-grey
as some enormous scrap of sheet metal
& wind grabs the world around the equator
I am most thankful then for knowing about
        the little gold hairs on your belly

Roblin's Mills

The mill was torn down last year
and stone's internal grey light
gives way to new green
a shading of surface colour
like the greenest apple of several
The spate of Marthas and Tabithas
        incessant Hirams and Josephs
is stemmed in the valley graveyard
where the censored quarrels of loving
and the hatred and by golly gusto
of a good crop of buckwheat and turnips
end naturally as an agreement between friends
        (in the sandy soil
that would grow nothing but weeds
or feed a few gaunt cattle) —
And the spring rain takes their bodies
a little deeper down each year
        and maybe the earliest settlers
some stern Martha or speechless Joseph
perhaps meet and mingle
        1,000 feet down —

And the story about the grist mill
rented in 1914 to a man named Taylor
by the last of the Roblin family
who demanded a share of the profits
that poured golden thru the flume
because the new miller knew his business:
        & the lighting alters
        here and now changes
to then and you can see
        how a bald man stood
sturdily indignant
        and spat on the floor
and stamped away so hard the flour
dust floated out from his clothes
like a white ghostly nimbus
around the red scorn
and the mill closed down —

        Those old ones
you can hear them on a rural party line
sometimes
        when the copper wires
sing before the number is dialed and
then your own words stall some distance
from the house you said them in
        lost in the 4th concession
        or dimension of wherever
        what happened still happens
        a lump in your throat
        an adam's apple half
        a mile down the road
        permits their voices
        to join living voices
        and float by
        on the party line sometimes
        and you hang up then
        so long now —

THE COUNTRY NORTH OF BELLEVILLE

Bush land scrub land —
        Cashel Township and Wollaston
Elzevir McClure and Dungannon
green lands of Weslemkoon Lake
where a man might have some
        opinion of what beauty
is and none deny him
           for miles —

Yet this is the country of defeat
where Sisyphus rolls a big stone
year after year up the ancient hills
picnicking glaciers have left strewn
with centuries' rubble
           backbreaking days
           in the sun and rain
when realization seeps slow in the mind
without grandeur or self-deception in
           noble struggle
of being a fool —

A country of quiescence and still distance
a lean land
        not like the fat south
with inches of black soil on
        earth's round belly —
And where the farms are
        it's as if a man stuck
both thumbs in the stony earth and pulled

           it apart
           to make room
enough between the trees
for a wife

and maybe some cows and
room for some
of the more easily kept illusions —
And where the farms have gone back
to forest
are only soft outlines
shadowy differences —
Old fences drift vaguely among the trees
a pile of moss-covered stones
gathered for some ghost purpose
has lost meaning under the meaningless sky
— they are like cities under water
and the undulating green waves of time
are laid on them—

This is the country of our defeat
and yet
during the fall plowing a man
might stop and stand in a brown valley of the furrows
and shade his eyes to watch for the same
red patch mixed with gold
that appears on the same
spot in the hills
year after year
and grow old
plowing and plowing a ten-acre field until
the convolutions run parallel with his own brain —

And this is a country where the young
leave quickly
unwilling to know what their fathers know
or think the words their mothers do not say —

Herschel Monteagle and Faraday
lakeland rockland and hill country
a little adjacent to where the world is

a little north of where the cities are and
sometime
we may go back there
                    to the country of our defeat
Wollaston Elzevir and Dungannon
and Weslemkoon Lake land
where the high townships of Cashel
                    McClure and Marmora once were —
But it's been a long time since
and we must enquire the way
        of strangers —

~~⌐

FIDEL CASTRO IN REVOLUTIONARY SQUARE

He begins to speak
about guns and drums and sugar
production higher this year
(a million people listening)
about impossible peace
and war and I wonder
how it was
with that young student
years ago in Havana drinking
with friends silently the colour
of Cuban April on his face
from flowers and the red earth
outside fading in the gold afternoon
I wonder about that young student
and speculate the exact moment
he sprang to his feet
stuttering with earnestness:
        "Listen to me
        we're going to take over
        all of us here in this room

the people here in this room
and all the people
we're going to take over the country"
The fragile intention flees
from face to face like fever
becomes a condition of existence
a thought to think when first
putting on your pants in the morning
and the faces gather around him
the whispering ghosts of justice
say to him "Fidel! Fidel!?"
and the high talk begins
And a stranger sits down then
shaken and sweating
not the same young student
not the same man
Ten years and three hours
later in 1964
the long speech ends
and it's "Fidel! Fidel!"
without any question at all
Everyone joins hands and sings together
a million voices and bodies
sway back and forth in the sunlight
and make some remark about being human
addressed to no one exactly
spoken to no imperialist
snarled at no invader
as natural as eating supper
that is able to touch the future
and fill an emptiness
and fills an emptiness in the future
Or else that's another illusion
something nice to believe in
and all of us need something
something to lift us from ourselves

a thing we touch that touches
a future we don't know
the continuity of people
a we/they and me/you concept
as saccharine as religion
to comfort a world of children
with proletarian lullabies
A million people move to the exits
under a sky empty of everything
returning to the fact of duration
and chicken hearts in nutritive solution
and glands living the good life
                         in a test tube
the great ambiguity the last cliché
And back at the shining Cadillac
we came in (Batista's old car)
under the side where I hadn't
noticed before the body
of a small dead animal

Cuba

Transient

Riding the boxcars out of Winnipeg in a
morning after rain so close to
the violent sway of fields it's
like running and running
naked with summer in your mouth and
the guy behind you grunts and says
"Got a smoke?"

Being a boy scarcely a moment and you
hear the rumbling iron roadbed singing

under the wheels at night and a door jerking open
mile after dusty mile riding into Regina with
the dust storm crowding behind you and
a guy you hardly even spoke to
nudges your shoulder chummily and says
"Got a smoke?"

Riding into the Crow's Nest mountains with
your first beard itching and a
hundred hungry guys fanning out thru
the shabby whistlestops for handouts and
not even a sandwich for two hundred miles
only the high mountains and knowing
what it's like to be not quite a child any
more and listening to the tough men
talk of women and talk of the way things are
in 1937

Riding down in the spit-grey sea-level morning
thru dockyard streets and dingy dowager houses
with ocean a jump away and the sky beneath you
in puddles on Water Street and an old Indian woman
pushing her yawning scratching daughter
onto a balcony to yell at the boy-man passing
"Want some fun? — come on up" — and the girl just
come from riding the shrieking bedspring bronco
all the up and down night to a hitchpost morning
full of mother and dirt and lice and
      hardly the place for a princess
      of the Coast Salish
            (My dove my little one
tonight there will be wine and drunken suitors
from the logging camps to pin you down
in the outlying lands of sleep
where all roads lead back to the home-village
and water may be walked on)

Stand in the swaying boxcar doorway
moving east away from the sunset and
after a while the eyes digest a country and
the belly perceives a mapmaker's vision
in dust and dirt on the face and hands here
its smell drawn deep thru the nostrils down
to the lungs and spurts thru blood stream
campaigns in the lower intestine
       and chants love songs to the kidneys
After a while there is no arrival and
no departure possible any more
you are where you were always going
and the shape of home is under your fingernails
the borders of yourself grown into certainty
the identity of forests that were always nameless
the selfhood of rivers that are changing always
the nationality of riding freight trains thru the depression
over long green plains and high mountain country
with the best and worst of a love that's not to be spoken
and a guy right behind you says then
"Got a smoke?"
You give him one and stand in the boxcar doorway
or looking out the window of a Montreal apartment
or running the machines in a Vancouver factory
you stand there growing older

TREES AT THE ARCTIC CIRCLE
(Salix Cordifolia — Ground Willow)

They are 18 inches long
or even less
crawling under rocks
grovelling among the lichens
bending and curling to escape

38

making themselves small
finding new ways to hide
Coward trees
I am angry to see them
like this
not proud of what they are
bowing to weather instead
careful of themselves
worried about the sky
afraid of exposing their limbs
like a Victorian married couple

I call to mind great Douglas firs
I see tall maples waving green
and oaks like gods in autumn gold
the whole horizon jungle dark
and I crouched under that continual night
But these
even the dwarf shrubs of Ontario
mock them
Coward trees

And yet — and yet —
their seed pods glow
like delicate grey earrings
their leaves are veined and intricate
like tiny parkas
They have about three months
to make sure the species does not die
and that's how they spend their time
unbothered by any human opinion
just digging in here and now
sending their roots down down down
And you know it occurs to me
                    about 2 feet under
those roots must touch permafrost

ice that remains ice forever
and they use it for their nourishment
they use death to remain alive

I see that I've been carried away
in my scorn of the dwarf trees
most foolish in my judgements
To take away the dignity
                of any living thing
even tho it cannot understand
                the scornful words
is to make life itself trivial
and yourself the Pontifex Maximus
                of nullity
I have been stupid in a poem
I will not alter the poem
but let the stupidity remain permanent
as the trees are
in a poem
the dwarf trees of Baffin Island

Pangnirtung

ARCTIC RHODODENDRONS

They are small purple surprises
in the river's white racket
and after you've seen them
a number of times
in water-places
where their silence seems
related to river-thunder
you think of them as "noisy flowers"
Years ago

it may have been
that lovers came this way
stopped in the outdoor hotel
to watch the water floorshow
and lying prone together
where the purged green
boils to a white heart
and the shore trembles
like a stone song
with bodies touching
flowers were their conversation
and love the sound of a colour
that lasts two weeks in August
and then dies
except for the three or four
I pressed in this letter
and send whispering to you

Pangnirtung

STILL LIFE IN A TENT
(Or, Tenting tonight in the old camp ground)

In a cave hollowed out in the rain
near a pile of ghostly groceries
and some books
The wind comes
within two feet of where I'm lying
then stops
waiting
and the canvas bulges

I have a slight fever
temperature of maybe 100

nothing to speak of
but no medicine here
And I have a small fear that changes
shape and size
when I consider what might happen
(canoe trip by sea to Pang
among the waving kelp lines
that anchor somebody's world
maybe the seal towns
or Erewhon and Atlantis
with Jonahsie nursing the motor
smiling but irritated
at me for making him
miss the good hunting weather
and myself sick in the bilge)

Waves rumble and rant now
on the still listening beach
pounding motherless bergs
to death on rocks
stranding the big calves
at tidal ebb
A clump of yellow flowers
I noticed this afternoon
must be straining their roots
in the windy twilit night
hoping to hold onto
their few home-inches
(like comic yellow flags
of a 40-acre duchy
between Russia and China)
Oh misery me misery me
I am sick as hell
and so sorry for me
touch my forehead
and swallow carefully

expecting it to hurt
smoke a cigarette
drink some coffee
wish it were brandy
hope for morning
and the big wind howls
Now a berg splits
inside/outside the tent
a dry white noise
wet dogs drift in
and out of hearing
I lie there fevered and
float a single thought out
into a night tinted
with day flowers in my mind
then send a second one
to join the first
and my thoughts travel together
in fevered fantasy
north of summer
with ice become a thousand-foot wall
so photo-real it might be
me both here and there
staring up and up
a fevered little man
at that cold altar
where June July and August
are a brief tremor
on god's thermometer
My blood burns and burns
with bells of systole and diastole
tolling over the northland
while I strike cross-capillary
with ham sandwich and thermos
to find the court of the Seal-King
where trader and blind explorer

fumbled along the kelp lines
to reach their graves in a blizzard
or came at last to drown

Here I am again
back from the court of the Seal-King
lying in bed with fever
and I'm so glad to be here
no matter what happens
— riding the wind to Pang
or being bored at Frobisher
(waiting for clearing weather)
I'm so glad to be here
with the chance that comes but once
to any man in his lifetime
to travel deep in himself
to meet himself as a stranger
at the northern end of the world
Now the bullying wind blows faster
the yellow flags rush seaward
the stones cry out like people
as my fever suddenly goes
and the huskies bark like hell
the huskies bark like hell

In a cave hollowed out in the rain
near a pile of ghostly groceries
and some books
morning soon

Kikastan Islands

When I Sat Down to Play the Piano

He cometh forth hurriedly from his tent
and looketh for a quiet sequestered vale
he carrieth a roll of violet toilet tissue
and a forerunner goeth ahead to do him honour
yclept a snotty-nosed Eskimo kid
He findeth a quiet glade among great stones
squatteth forthwith and undoeth trousers
Irrational Man by Wm. Barrett in hand
while the other dismisseth mosquitoes
and beginneth the most natural of natural functions
buttocks balanced above the boulders
Then
      dogs[1]
         Dogs[3]
            DOGS[12]
                  all shapes and sizes
all colours and religious persuasion
a plague of dogs rushing in
having been attracted by the philosophic climate
and being wishful to learn about existential dogs
and denial of the self with regard to bitches
But let's call a spade a shovel
therefore there I am I am I think that is
surrounded by a dozen dozen fierce Eskimo dogs
with an inexplicable (to me) appetite
for human excrement
                  Dear Ann Landers
what would you do?
                  Dear Galloping Gourmet
what would *you* do
                  in a case like this?
Well I'll tell you
NOT A DAMN THING
You just squat there cursing hopelessly

while the kid throws stones
and tries to keep them off and out from under
as a big black husky dashes in
swift as an enemy submarine
white teeth snapping at the anus
I shriek
      and shriek
      (the kid laughs)
      and hold onto my pants
      sans dignity
      sans intellect
      sans Wm. Barrett
      and damn near sans anus
Stand firm little Eskimo kid
it giveth candy if I had any
it giveth a dime in lieu of same
STAND FIRM
Oh avatar of Olympian excellence
noble Eskimo youth do your stuff
Zeus in the Arctic dog pound
Montcalm at Quebec
Horatius at the bridge
Leonidas at Thermopylae
Custer's last stand at Little Big Horn
"KEEP THEM DAMN DOGS OFF
YOU MISERABLE LITTLE BRAT!"

Afterwards
Achilles retreateth without honour
unzippered and sullen
and sulketh in his tent till next time appointed
his anus shrinketh
he escheweth all forms of laxative and physick meanwhile
and prayeth for constipation
addresseth himself to the Eskimo brat miscalled
      "Lo tho I walk thru the valley of

the shadowy kennels
in the land of permanent ice cream
I will fear no huskies
for thou art with me
and slingeth thy stones forever and ever
thou veritable David
Amen"

PS Next time I'm gonna take a gun

Kikastan Islands

~~⌒

What Do the Birds Think?

Are they exiles here from the rest of the world?
Déjà vu past egg and atom
from the yellow Sahara-ocean
or farmlands in Ontario
a witness   hanging   painted
in the rural blue
while a plowman half a mile down
in the dark field with a snoring tractor
moves in circular sleep?
Or exiles from the apple country
where Macs and Spies plop soft
on wet ground in slow autumn days
with the rotten tangy odour
of cider rising on moon-wept nights?
Have they lists and a summary
of things elsewhere and
remember the crimson racket
encountering tropic strangers
or nests of an old absence
lined with a downy part of themselves

far south?
And being south do they think sometimes
of the rain and mists of Baffin
and long migrations wingtip to wingtip
a mile high
and mate to mate in the lift and tremble
of windy muscles pushing them
pushing them where?
And do they ever
an arrow leader pointing the way
touch wearily down on ships passing?
— "Rest here a while and go on!"
(Forgotten in the hurry
of their streaming generations
another captain
called Noah
& Bjarni Herjolfsson
in horned helmet
and the sweeps' silver lifting
to a luring Hyperborean ocean
or whaling ships' myopic stumbling
from dull wave to dull wave and the
paint of the bright over-the-horizon-gazing
woman flaked with salt)
How are we kept here
by what bonds
are we always exiles
a chirping roar in the silence
of foxes and watery romp of walrus
in the long sea lands
or perched on rubbery muskeg
like blue teacups
or lost brown mittens
by what agency of restlessness
in the driftwood heart?
Until on a day the eggs hatch

and the young are trained to endurance
ice rattles the shroud of summer
the flight plans sent
the log book sand is scribbled on
"Goodbye — we are going — Hurry"
and mounting a shaft of sunlight
or the mizzen mast of the sky
they climb and go
And that is the way it is?
Except perhaps I wonder
do they ever
remember down there in the southland
Cumberland Sound
and the white places
of Baffin
that I will remember
soon?

Pangnirtung

THE COUNTRY OF THE YOUNG

A.Y. Jackson for instance
83 years old
halfway up a mountain
standing in a patch of snow
to paint a picture that says
"Look here
You've never seen this country
it's not the way you thought it was
Look again"
And boozy traders
lost in a dream of money
crews of homesick seamen

moored to a China-vision
hunting the North West Passage
they didn't see it either
The colours I mean
for they're not bright Gauguin
or blazing Vincent
not even Brueghel's "Hunters in the Snow"
where you can get lost
and found in five minutes
— but the original colour-matrix
that after a giant's heartbeat
lighted the maple forests
in the country south
You have to stoop a little
bend over and then look up
—dull orange on a cliff face
that says iron deposits
olive leaves of the ground willow
with grey silver catkins
minute wild flower beacons
sea blue as the world's eye —
And you can't be looking for something else
money or a night's lodging on earth
a stepping stone to death maybe
or you'll never find the place
hear an old man's voice
in the country of the young
that says
            "Look here — "

Pangnirtung

~~⌒

DEAD SEAL

He looks like a fat little old man
an "Old Bill" sort of face
both wise and senile at the same time
with an anxious to please expression
                    in fact a clown
which is belied on account of the dark slow worm
of blood crawling down his forehead
that precludes laughter
or being anything but a dead animal
tho perhaps part of a fur coat

Often I want to pet something
that looks like this
(and been warned the Eskimo dogs are dangerous)
which appeals to me on common ground i.e.
they unsure of what being an animal consists of
I equally unsure of what a human being is supposed to be
(despite the legal and moral injunctions that say
                    "Thou Shalt Not"
nobody says or is likely to say with real conviction
                    "Thou Shalt — go ahead and Shalt"
                    or "shall" as the case may be)
On the other hand it would be ridiculous
to pat the head of a dead seal
touch the wet blood that streams back from the boat
a feather of smoky brown in the water widening
into a crude trailing isosceles triangle
with mathematically impossible fish
re-tracing the seal's ghost past not
knowing they're involved in anything

And here he is now
                    casually taking a nap
with flippers like futile baby hands

and clown look of just pretending
        I shan't wake him
for it would be disgusting to touch the blood
and it's unnecessary to prove anything
even to myself
        Then change my mind
        "I (damn well) Shalt"
— reach out as if the head were electric
with a death-taboo invisibly attached
dark and dank-cold with the hair on it
sticky where the bullet touched
            less gently
smooth elsewhere like an intimate part
        of the human body
that must be touched with delight in living
not curiosity and defiance of breaking rules
— But I am no hunter
        of any kind
go back to the tent
        to sit for a few minutes
inside the white canvas blindfold and wonder
what got into me?

Kikastan Islands

THE WINEMAKER'S BEAT-ÉTUDE

I am picking wild grapes last year
in a field
        dragging down great lianas of vine
tearing at 20 feet of heavy infinite purple
having a veritable tug-o-war with Bacchus
who grins at me delightedly in the high branches
of one of those stepchild appletrees

unloved by anything but tent caterpillars
and ghosts of old settlers
become such strangers here
I am thinking what the grapes are thinking
become part of their purple mentality
that is
    I am satisfied with the sun and
eventual fermenting bubble-talk together
then transformed and glinting with coloured lights in
    a GREAT JEROBOAM
that booms inside from the land beyond the world
In fact
I am satisfied with my own shortcomings letting
myself happen then
       I'm surrounded by Cows
black and white ones with tails
At first I'm uncertain how to advise them
in mild protest or frank manly invective
then realize that the cows are right
it's me that's the trespasser
      Of course they are curious
perhaps wish to see me perform
      I moo off key
      I bark like a man
      laugh like a dog
      and talk like God
      hoping
they'll go away so Bacchus and I can get on with it
Then I get logical thinking if there was ever a
feminine principle cows are it and why not but
what would so many females want?
I address them like Brigham Young hastily
"No, that's out! I won't do it!
      Absolutely not!"
Contentment steals back among all this femininity
thinking cows are together so much they must be nearly

all lesbians fondling each other's dugs by moonlight why
Sappho's own star-reaching soul shines inward and outward
from the soft Aegean islands in these eyes and
I am dissolved like a salt lick instantly oh

        Sodium chloride!

        Prophylactic acid!

        Gamma particles (in suspension)!

        Aftershave lotion!

        Rubbing alcohol!

           suddenly

I become the whole damn feminine principle so
happily noticing little tendrils of affection steal
out from each to each unshy honest encompassing
golden calves in Israel and slum babies in Canada and
a millionaire's brat left squalling on the toilet seat in
Rockefeller Center

        Oh my sisters
        I give purple milk!

HOMBRE

    — Met briefly in Havana
among the million Cubans waiting
Fidel's speech on May Day 1964
under a million merciless suns
He came around and shook hands
with the foreign visitors
a guy who looked like a service station attendant
in his olive drab fatigues and beret
but with the beard and black cigar
the resemblance ended
— the Argentine doctor and freedom fighter
Che Guevara
And I remember thinking the North Vietnamese ladies

54

looked especially flower-like beside him
I remember his grip particularly
firm but perfunctory
half politician and half revolutionary
for he had many hands to shake that day

Later he disappeared from Cuba
and there were rumours of quarrels
between himself and Castro
and US newspapers asked nervously
"Where is Che Guevara?"
Then Havana Radio reported Guevara
had joined guerrillas in "a South American country"
but the US expressed some small doubt
about the reliability of Havana Radio
while I thought of him — shaking hands

Back home in Canada I remembered Guevara
along with structural details of Cuban girls
the Grand Hotel at Camaguey with roosters
yammering into my early morning sleep
an all-night walk in Havana streets with a friend
a mad jeep-ride over the Sierra Maestras
where sea-raiders attacked a coastal sugar mill
and Playa Giron which is the "Bay of Pigs"
where the dead men have stopped caring
and alligators hiss in the late afternoon
Again May Day in Havana 1964
with a red blaze of flowers and banners
and Castro talking solemnly to his nation
a million people holding hands and singing
strange to think of this in Canada
And I remember Che Guevara
a man who made dreams something
he could hold in his hands both hands
saying "Hiya" or whatever they say in Spanish

to the flower-like Vietnamese ladies
cigar tilted into his own trademark
of the day when rebels swarmed out
of Oriente Province down from the mountains

"Where is Che Guevara?" is answered:
deep in Bolivian jungles leading his guerrillas
from cave to cave with scarlet cockatoos screaming
the Internationale around his shoulders
smoking a black cigar and wearing a beret
(like a student in Paris on a Guggenheim)
his men crawling under hundred-foot trees
where giant snakes mate in masses of roots
and men with infected wounds moan for water
while Guevara leads his men into an ambush
and out again just like in the movies
but the good guy loses and the bad guys always win
and the band plays the Star-Spangled Banner
Well it is over
Guevara is dead now and whether the world
is any closer to freedom because
of Che's enormous dream is not to be known
the bearded Argentine doctor who translated
that dream to a handshake among Bolivian peasants
and gave himself away free to those who wanted him
his total self and didn't keep any
I remember the news reports from Bolivia
how he was wounded   captured   executed   cremated
but first they cut off his fingers
for fingerprint identification later
in case questions should be asked
and I remember his quick hard handshake
in Havana among the tiny Vietnamese ladies
and seem to hold ghostlike in my own hand
five bloody fingers
of Che Guevara

WATCHING TRAINS

Indian boys at Nakina and Sioux Lookout
from tent towns in the bush
and blueberry shacks by a railway siding
($1.50 a basket in bargain summer)
with schoolmarm passenger distributing
replicas of the new Canadian flag
Boys with their mouths open
some missing part supplied by trains
Thought will not come to them nor speech
they have no words for department stores
or pictographs for elevators going fifty
miles an hour into the sky
They watch the train
dumbfound as newfallen snow
      blank eyes and blank minds
that do not follow down the whispering rails
or think of anything
until the train goes
and birds dispute the ownership of silence

Hours or miles
later in the snowbush
with summer gone
they hear a diesel hoot
like blood that shrieks inside their toenails
trains
inside their inward eye
from all directions bearing down on them
from deadfalls under scrub cedar
and burned pine skeletons
and traplines where the red-eyed weasel
snarls in a wire noose
and foxes gnaw their forelegs
free from steel

the trains
converge from snowhung poplar coverts
mooseyards and small creeks
their bubble music choked with ice
the diesels vector in
And rails run down the day's horizon
a white eye slants on hogback hills
thru midnight zero pullmans pass
and spike their echoes to the trees . . .

Trains
          things
                    thought itself
no capital letters tattooed presto
on people
like Mr. Tecumseh and Mr. Hiawatha
or Joe Something
faces are faces
The skulls contain
pictures of things
woodsmoke messages
the melted circle of snow
around living trees
old loved rifles
the price of blueberries
people
happening memories
maybe death
and trains
trains
And will see them like small glory
among snarling dogs and chewed bones in the snow
as wind invades the tarpaper mansions
till June and the bush raspberries come

Dark Landscape

For a week the flies have been terrible
not medium-size houseflies
but heavy foreboding buzzard-creatures
dive-bombing thru clouds of insecticide
knocking dishes from shelves
and body checking the furniture
Lying awake in darkness I hear them
blundering thru night's frontiers
frantic about something
antennae picking up signals outside the house
as if there was a point to existence
other than personal
as if they registered a protest
No sun or wind on the grey lake
all morning and thru the long afternoon
summer cottagers gone
a pair of tall elms
dead long since from dutch elm disease
are indistinguishable from other trees
their small bones leafless
Well I've no doubt weather
does influence human mood and
when it rains people are seldom optimists
in middle age the body itself
slows to contemplate nothingness
seasonal metrics stagger and jerk to a halt
mandolins in grass roots end
winter is coming
I sit stupefied
waiting . . .

Across the sky a flight of geese
goes sweeping to the continental vanishing point
sends a honking cry down here now

fading to an almost inaudible mockery
as they reach towards lands of the sun
All this brings on an opposite reaction
and I laugh I must laugh
it's too pat too trite and too goddam soon
too easy to turn down the music and wait
or alternatively
brush reality aside with physical action?
But "to live a life is not to cross a field"?
Is it then to cross many fields
wear blinkers and cultivate a cheerful outlook?
With brain relinquished the body takes over?
And I laugh and span the continent with a letter
write a dozen letters to Vancouver
Vancouver   Montreal   and Toronto
drink a glass of wine and knock the bottle over
down the dregs and stain my guts with purple
think about a girl who couldn't love me
(oh impossible and inconceivable to love you
as she passionately mentioned) and I laugh
and think — for life to have a meaning
or even several meanings well it's funny
tho one of them is getting rather drunken
in the afterbirth of youth and maybe wine and
maybe spring comes on forever spring goes on forever
said Aladdin to the jinn jinn gin

And maybe down below the lowest floorboards
where the dead flies buzz and blunder
a girl will whisper maybe yes I do
yes I do you euphemistic bastard
me as shouldn't me as oughtn't on accounta
you don't take women serious as you really
ought to do you
don't take livin serious
                    Yes I do yes I do

tho I'm gettin rather elderly for crossin fields in winter
is serious as anything and hemispheres take longer
and elms are dying momently as I say this to you
    and flies are something terrible
    and mushroom clouds likewise
    and there's them that die of livin
    and there's them that joy in dyin
    and there's agony and screamin
    and all I have is laughter
    all I have is wine and laughter
    and the spring came on forever
    the spring comes on forever
        Yes I do

Roblin Lake

THE DRUNK TANK

A man keeps hammering at the door
(he is so noisy it makes my ears ache),
yelling monotonously, "Let me outa here!"
A caged light bulb floats on the ceiling,
where a dung fly circles round and round,
and there is a greasy brown mattress,
too small for the bolted-down steel bunk,
and a high barred window permitting
fungus darkness to creep in the room's corners.
The man keeps hammering at the door
until a guard comes:
"I just happen to know the mayor in this town,"
he tells the guard,
"and it's gonna be too bad for you
if you keep me locked up here."
The guard laughs and turns away.
"It's no use," I tell my cell mate.

"Just wait until morning.
Then we'll be up in magistrate's court,
and being drunk isn't a very serious — "
"Who are you?" the man asks me.
"I don't know you — "
"I'm your friend," I say to him,
"and I've been your friend a long time.
Don't you remember?"
"I don't know you at all!" he screams.
"Stay away from me!"
"If that's the way you feel about it," I say,
and suddenly I'm not so sure as I was
— memory is a funny thing isn't it?
"Please sit down and wait until morning,"
I say to him reasonably —
Don't you think that was the right thing to say?
But he turns his back and hammers on the door:
"Guard! Guard! I want a cell by myself!
You've put a crazy man in here with me!"
He is so noisy.
And I watch him pounding on the black steel door,
a patch of sweat spreading on his back,
and his bald spot glistening —
He looks at me over his shoulder,
terrified:
and I spread my hands flat to show him
I have nothing but good intentions.
"Stay away from me! Stay away!"
He backs off into a corner shaking,
while I sit down on the bunk
to wait for morning.
And I think:
this is my friend,
I know it is my friend,
and I say to him,
"Aren't you my friend?"
But there he is at the door again,
he is so noisy . . .

SERGEANT JACKSON

In the long grass lying
there in 1944
hating that sergeant for thinking
three stripes made him so superior
he could get away with anything
peering thru tall grass at him
hoping his face might alter
flush or grow pale
and he'd double over with agony
from the force in my eyes
VOODOO thoughts
of an RCAF airman
— trying to make the self-important
bastard throw up his dinner
contract any ailment untrivial
like a permanent dose of clap
or imaginary fleas
approx. the size of rats
A big eagle circling the sun
with eyes a golden snare
looped round the green valley
snow peaks overhead
dust blowing across the airfield
the Skeena sailing past
railway tracks heading for Rupert
48-hour-pass cancelled
myself stuck there forever
where even Japs would be welcome
but they have more sense
and no woman for miles
and no woman for centuries
All this a long time ago:
I remember grass tickling my chin
mountains near and high and far away

axe blows smashing at silence
Indian canoes on the Skeena
totem poles and some friends
nothing is lost
That sergeant?
I convince no one now
even myself
that I hated him
but my hate was holy and beautiful then
and life got damned interesting
a sword was laid across the month of August
it worked like 100 proof booze
and made the landscape glow
black runways where the planes landed
writhed like snakes in the heat haze
but no one else noticed
how the edges of things sharpened
and quivered like fine gold lettering
on pages of cracked parchment
and the crummy barracks lit up
during poker games
and left that time photographed
in the dumb compartments of memory
where love was slowly becoming possible

Roblin's Mills (2)

The wheels stopped
and the murmur of voices
behind the flume's tremble
stopped
        and the wind-high ships
that sailed from Rednersville
to the sunrise ports of Europe
are delayed somewhere
in a toddling breeze
The black millpond
turns an unreflecting eye
to look inward
like an idiot child
locked in the basement
when strangers come
whizzing past on the highway
above the dark green valley
a hundred yards below
The mill space is empty
even stones are gone
where hands were shaken
and walls enclosed laughter
saved up and brought here
from the hot fields
where all stories
are rolled into one
And white dust floating
above the watery mumble
and bright human sounds
to shimmer among the pollen
where bees dance now
Of all these things
no outline remains
no shadow on the soft air
no bent place in the heat glimmer
where the heavy walls pressed
And some of those who vanished

lost children of the time
kept after school
left alone in a graveyard
who may not change
or ever grow six inches
in one hot summer
or turn where the great herons
graze the sky's low silver
— stand between the hours
in a rotting village
near the weed-grown eye
that looks into itself
deep in the black crystal
that holds and contains
the substance of shadows
manner and custom
          of the inarticulate
departures and morning rumours
gestures and almost touchings
announcements and arrivals
gossip of someone's marriage
when a girl or tired farm woman
whose body suddenly blushes
beneath a faded house dress
with white expressionless face
turns to her awkward husband
to remind him of something else
The black millpond
                    holds them
movings and reachings and fragments
the gear and tackle of living
under the water eye
all things laid aside
               discarded
                    forgotten
but they had their being once
and left a place to stand on

About Being a Member of Our Armed Forces

Remember the early days of the phony war
when men were zombies and women were CWACs
and they used wooden rifles on the firing range?
Well I was the sort of soldier you couldn't trust
with a wooden rifle
and when they gave me a wooden bayonet
life was fraught with peril for my brave comrades
including the sergeant-instructor
I wasn't exactly a soldier tho
only a humble airman
who kept getting demoted
                        and demoted
                                    and demoted
to the point where I finally saluted civilians
And when they trustingly gave me a Sten gun
Vancouver should have trembled in its sleep
for after I fired a whole clip of bullets
at some wild ducks under Burrard Bridge
(on guard duty at midnight)
they didn't fly away for five minutes
trying to decide if there was any danger
Not that the war was funny
I took it and myself quite seriously
the way a squirrel in a treadmill does
too close to tears for tragedy
too far from the banana peel for laughter
and I didn't blame anyone for being there
that wars happened wasn't anybody's fault then

Now I think it is

LAMENT FOR THE DORSETS

(Eskimos extinct in the 14th century AD)

Animal bones and some mossy tent rings
scrapers and spearheads   carved ivory swans
all that remains of the Dorset giants
who drove the Vikings back to their long ships
talked to spirits of earth and water
— a picture of terrifying old men
so large they broke the backs of bears
so small they lurk behind bone rafters
in the brain of modern hunters
among good thoughts and warm things
and come out at night
to spit on the stars

The big men with clever fingers
who had no dogs and hauled their sleds
over the frozen northern oceans
awkward giants
               killers of seal
they couldn't compete with little men
who came from the west with dogs
Or else in a warm climatic cycle
the seals went back to cold waters
and the puzzled Dorsets scratched their heads
with hairy thumbs around 1350 AD
— couldn't figure it out
went around saying to each other
plaintively
      "What's wrong? What happened?
      Where are the seals gone?"
And died

Twentieth-century people
apartment dwellers

executives of neon death
warmakers with things that explode
— they have never imagined us in their future
how could we imagine them in the past
squatting among the moving glaciers
six hundred years ago
with glowing lamps?
As remote or nearly
as the trilobites and swamps
when coal became
or the last great reptile hissed
at a mammal the size of a mouse
that squeaked and fled

Did they ever realize at all
what was happening to them?
Some old hunter with one lame leg
a bear had chewed
sitting in a caribou-skin tent
— the last Dorset?
Let's say his name was Kudluk
and watch him sitting there
carving 2-inch ivory swans
for a dead grand-daughter
taking them out of his mind
the places in his mind
where pictures are
He selects a sharp stone tool
to gouge a parallel pattern of lines
on both sides of the swan
holding it with his left hand
bearing down and transmitting
his body's weight
from brain to arm and right hand
and one of his thoughts
turns to ivory

The carving is laid aside
in beginning darkness
at the end of hunger
and after a while wind
blows down the tent and snow
begins to cover him

After 600 years
the ivory thought
is still warm

WILDERNESS GOTHIC

Across Roblin Lake, two shores away,
they are sheathing the church spire
with new metal. Someone hangs in the sky
over there from a piece of rope,
hammering and fitting God's belly-scratcher,
working his way up along the spire
until there's nothing left to nail on —
Perhaps the workman's faith reaches beyond:
touches intangibles, wrestles with Jacob,
replacing rotten timber with pine thews,
pounds hard in the blue cave of the sky,
contends heroically with difficult problems of
gravity, sky navigation and mythopoeia,
his volunteer time and labour donated to God,
minus sick benefits of course on a non-union job —

Fields around are yellowing into harvest,
nestling and fingerling are sky and water borne,
death is yodelling quiet in green woodlots,
and bodies of three young birds have disappeared
in the sub-surface of the new county highway —

That picture is incomplete, part left out
that might alter the whole Dürer landscape:
gothic ancestors peer from medieval sky,
dour faces trapped in photograph albums escaping
to clop down iron roads with matched greys:
work-sodden wives groping inside their flesh
for what keeps moving and changing and flashing
beyond and past the long frozen Victorian day.
A sign of fire and brimstone? A two-headed calf
born in the barn last night? A sharp female agony?
An age and a faith moving into transition,
the dinner cold and new-baked bread a failure,
deep woods shiver and water drops hang pendant,
double-yolked eggs and the house creaks a little —
Something is about to happen. Leaves are still.
Two shores away, a man hammering in the sky.
Perhaps he will fall.

THE RUNNERS

*"It was when Leif was with King Olaf Tryggvason, and he bade him proclaim
Christianity to Greenland, that the King gave him two Gaels; the man's
name was Haki, and the woman's Haekia. The King advised Leif to have
recourse to these people, if he should stand in need of fleetness, for they
were swifter than deer. Erick and Leif had tendered Karlsefni the services of
this couple. Now when they had sailed past Marvel-Strands (to the New
World) they put the Gaels ashore, and directed them to run to the southward,
and investigate the nature of the country, and return again before the end
of the third half-day."*
                    (from *Erick the Red's Saga*)

Brother, the wind of this place is cold,
and hills under our feet tremble,
the forests are making magic against us —

I think the land knows we are here,
I think the land knows we are strangers.
Let us stay close to our friend the sea,
or cunning dwarves at the roots of darkness
shall seize and drag us down —

Sister, we must share our strength between us,
until the heat of our bodies makes a single flame:
while the moon sees only one shadow
and the sun knows only our double heartbeat,
and the rain does not come between —

Brother, I am afraid of this dark place,
I am hungry for the home islands,
and wind blowing the waves to coloured spray,
I am sick for the sun —

Sister, we must not think those thoughts again,
for three-half days have gone by,
and we must return to the ship.
If we are away longer,
the Northmen will beat us with thongs,
until we cry for death —
Why do you stare at nothing?

Brother, a cold wind touched me,
tho I stand in your arms' circle:
perhaps the Northmen's runes have found us,
the runes they carve on wood and stone.
I am afraid of this dark land,
ground mist that makes us half ghosts,
and another silence inside silence . . .
But there are berries and fish here,
and small animals by the sea's edge
that crouch and tremble and listen . . .
If we join our thoughts to the silence,
if our trails join the animal trails,
and the sun remembers what the moon forgets . . .
Brother it comes to me now,

the long ship must sail without us,
we stay here —

Sister, we should die slowly,
the beasts would gnaw at our bodies,
the rains whiten our bones.
The Northmen's runes are strong magic,
the runes would track us down,
tho we keep on running
past the Land of Flat Stones
over the Marvel-Strands
beyond the country of great trees . . .
Tho we ran to the edge of the world,
our masters would track us down —

Brother, take my hand in your hand,
this part of ourselves between us
while we run together,
over the stones of the sea-coast,
this much of ourselves is our own:
while rain cries out against us,
and darkness swallows the evening,
and morning moves into stillness,
and mist climbs to our throats,
while we are running,
while we are running —

Sister —

Over the Hills in the Rain, My Dear

We are walking back from the Viking site,
dating ten centuries ago
(it must be about four miles),
and rain beats on us,
soaks our clothes,
runs into our shoes,
makes white pleats in our skin,
turns hair into decayed seaweed:
and I think sourly that drowning
on land is a helluva slow way to die.
I walk faster than my wife,
then have to stop and wait for her:
"It isn't much farther,"
I say encouragingly
and note that our married life
is about to end in violence,
judging from her expressionless expression.
Again I slop into the lead,
then wait in the mud till she catches up,
thinking, okay, I'll say something complimentary:
"You sure are a sexy lookin mermaid dear!"
That don't go down so good either,
and she glares at me like a female vampire
resisting temptation badly:
at which point I've forgotten
all about the rain,
trying to manufacture
a verbal comfort station,
a waterproof two-seater.
We squelch miserably into camp
about half an hour later,
strip down like white shrivelled slugs,
waving snail horns at each other,
cold sexless antennae

assessing the other ridiculous creature —
And I begin to realize
one can't use a grin like a bandaid
or antidote for reality,
at least not all the time:
and maybe it hurts my vanity
to know she feels sorry for me,
she's sorry for *me*,
and I don't know why:
but to be a fool
is sometimes
my own good luck.

L'Anse aux Meadows, Nfld.

~⁓

DETAIL

The ruined stone house
has an old apple tree
left there by the farmer
whatever else he took with him
It bears fruit every year
gone wild and wormy
with small bitter apples
nobody eats
even children know better
I passed that way on the road
to Trenton twice a month
all winter long
noticing how the apples clung
in spite of hurricane winds
sometimes with caps of snow
little golden bells
And perhaps none of the other

travellers looked that way
but I make no parable of them
they were there and that's all
For some reason I must remember
and think of the leafless tree
and its fermented fruit
one week in late January
when wind blew down the sun
and earth shook like a cold room
no one could live in
with zero weather
soundless golden bells
alone in the storm

MARRIED MAN'S SONG

When he makes love to the young girl
what does the middle-aged long-married
man say to himself and the girl?
— that lovers live and desk clerks perish?

When neons flash the girl into light and shadow
the room vanishes and all those others
guests who checked out long ago
are smiling
and only the darkness of her may be touched
only the whiteness looked at
she stands above him as a stone goddess
weeping tears and honey
she is half his age and far older
and how can a man tell his wife this?

Later they'll meet in all politeness
not quite strangers but never friends

and hands touched elsewhere may shake together
with brush of fingers and casual eyes
and the cleanser cleans to magic whiteness
and love survives in the worst cologne
(But not girls' bodies that turn black leather)
for all believe in the admen's lies

In rare cases among the legions of married men
such moments of shining have never happened
and whether to praise such men for their steadfast virtue
or condemn them as fools for living without magic
answer can hardly be given

There are rooms for rent in the outer planets
and neons blaze in Floral Sask
we live with death but it's life we die with
in the blossoming earth where springs the rose
In house and highway in town and country
what's given is paid for blood gifts are sold
the stars' white fingers unscrew the light bulbs
the bill is due and the desk clerk wakes
outside our door the steps are quiet
light comes and goes from a ghostly sun
where only the darkness may be remembered
and the rest is gone

DEAD MARCH FOR SERGEANT MACLEOD

(Seventy years old, wounded and returning to England from Quebec with the corpse of General Wolfe in 1759)

The sea outside is the river
St. Lawrence and the boxed corpse
once General Wolfe and the wide mouth
of the gulf is a womb of death and the lap
lap lap of water is memory memory
of drums and guns the smoking guns
outside Quebec the dead are shovelled
and buried each with a lithograph
in his head and heart and brain
of the last thought the last glass
of wine the last woman the last
small lead ball growing and growing
and becoming smaller being nothing
And what about you General   sir
in a coffin in the hold of the Royal
William draped in a flag does Gray's
Elegy still seem very important now
to you in your pine box at any rate
what about God whose existence is not
beyond doubt puttering around
in a workshop jammed with hypotheses
you with your weak body and chinless
face fixed fast with its last commands
like stones shied back from nowhere?
And you Sergeant MacLeod
are there wars ready
and waiting for you to arrive adrenalin
stored in your head musket balls
firing indiscriminate pop pop pop?
Old killer on the battlefields of Europe
old amputator of arms and legs and daylight
staring at Wolfe's corpse admiringly

what do you say Sergeant
any advice for new recruits now
and how do you speak to Generals even
if they're dead and don't hear a word
only the waves outside going lap lap lap
idiot music idiot questions idiot God?
— rockabye Skye baby rockabye home
inside the wooden walls of the womb of things
where we have been where we are going
when we are not —

THE HORSEMAN OF AGAWA
(Indian rock-painting under the cliffs of Lake Superior)

It's spring and the steel platforms tourists usually stand on
are not installed yet so we take our chances
but I have to abandon my beer and use both hands for safety
We clamber down rocks unsteady as children
reach slanting stone ledges under the hundred-foot walls
my wife skipping ahead so nimbly I'm jealous of her
and say "Wait for me, dammit" but she won't
then take my shoes off and go barefoot

She sees the painting first and calls "Here!"
her face flattens and dissolves into no expression
I balance myself beside her on the tilted ledge
that slides off into deep water and the rock hurts my feet
but I feel the same way she does as the rock horseman canters
by two feet from my nose forever or nearly
The painted horseman rides over four moons (or suns) on his trail
whose meaning must be a four-day journey somewhere
the red iron oxide faded from Lake Superior storms
and maybe two hundred years since the Ojibway artist
        stood there

balanced above water like us
and drew with his fingers on the stone canvas
with fish eggs or bear grease to make the painting permanent
pitting fish eggs and bear grease against eternity
which is kind of ludicrous or kind of beautiful I guess

I have too many thoughts about the horseman
I might select one and say this is a signpost this painting
(in fact I've just done that)
a human-as-having-babies signpost
but also dammit part of the spirit
a thought taken out from inside the head and carefully left here
like saying I love you to stone
I think that after the Ojibway are all dead
and all the bombs in the white world have fizzed into harmlessness
the ghost of one inept hunter who always got lost
and separated from his friends because he had a lousy sense
        of direction
that man can come here to get his bearings calling out
to his horse his dog or himself because he's alone
in the fog in the night in the rain in his mind and say
"My friends where are you?"
and the rock walls will seize his voice
and break it into a million amplified pieces of echoes
that will find the ghosts of his friends in the tombs of their dust

But I mistrust the mind-quality that tempts me
to embroider and exaggerate things
                         I just watch my wife's face
she is quiet as she generally is because I do most of the talking
it is forty years old and has felt the pain of children
the pettiness of day-to-day living and getting thousands of meals
but standing on the rock face of Lake Superior
it is not lessened in any way
with a stillness of depth that reaches where I can't follow
all other thoughts laid aside in her brain

on her face I see the Ojibway horseman painting the rock with
      red fingers
and he speaks to her as I could not
in pictures without handles of words
into feeling into being here by direct transmission
from the stranded Ojibway horseman
And I change it all back into words again for that's the best I can do
but they only point the way we came from for who knows where
      we are
under the tall stone cliffs with water dripping down on us
or returned from a long journey and calling out to our friends

But the rock blazes into light when we leave the place
or else the sun shines somewhere else and I didn't notice it
and my secret knowing is knowing what she knows
and can't say and I can only indicate
reclaim my half-empty beer and drink it and tie my shoes
follow her up the tangled rocks past the warning sign for strangers
and wait till she turns around

～⌒

THE BEAVERS OF RENFREW

By day
chain saws stencil the silence in my head
black quotes appear on the red brain
Across glacial birth marks old Jake
Loney is cutting his winter wood,
tongue drowned in a chaw of tobacco —
The belly button pond at one
end of the farm brims
full its cockleshell three acres:
— tonight the beavers are back,
and work their swing shift

under the moon.
Sometimes at low earthen dams
where the pouring spillway empties,
they stand upright in a pride of being,
holding rainbow trout like silver thoughts,
or pale gold Indian girls
arriving here intact from bone cameras
ten thousand ancestors ago,
before letting them spin down the moonlight
rapids as mortal lures
for drowned fishermen —
Among the beaver lodges
I stand unable to sleep,
but cannot stay awake
while poplar and birch fall around me.
I am not mistaken for a tree,
but almost totally ignored,
pissed on by mistake occasionally —
Standing here long enough,
seeing the gentle bodies moving
close to what they truly are,
I wonder what screwed-up philosophy,
what claim to a god's indulgence
made men decide their own importance?
And what is great music and art
but an alibi for murderers?
Perhaps in the far-off beginnings
of things they made a pact with men,
dammed the oceans for us,
chewed a hole in the big log bridge
wedged between Kamchatka and Alaska,
tore open the Mediterranean,
parted the Red Sea for Moses,
drowned Atlantis and the myth
of original sin
in the great salt womb of the sea —

And why?
Because they pitied men.
To the wet animal shivering in a tree
they said
        "Come on down —
                        It's all right."
And he shinnied down with hairless
purple behind pointed east for heat,
tail between hind legs,
humbly standing on all fours,
touching his forelock muttering,
"Yessir yessir thank'ee kindly,"
but not knowing how to speak yet of course —
Beaver looked at this dripping creature
a miserable biological dead end:
but every failure has flashes of genius
exploding out of imminent death
and the man listened
to an agreement of the water beings
and land beings together
which men have forgotten since:
the secret of staying completely still,
allowing ourselves to catch up
with the shadow just ahead of us
we have lost,
when the young world was a cloudy room
drifting thru morning stillness —
But the rest of it
I have forgotten,
and the gentle beaver will not remind us:
standing upright at their earthen dams
holding the moonlit reins of water,
at peace with themselves —

"Why not make a left turn in
time and just stay here,"

I said next day to old Jake Loney,
"instead of going on to the planets?"
The chain saw bucked in his hands,
chewing out chunks of pine that toppled
and scarred the air with green absence.
Far off a beaver tail slapped water,
a bird looked for the tree that was gone —
Old Jake's cheek bulged its chaw of tobacco —
"Well, why not?" I said argumentatively,
before he could spit,
                    "Why not?"
And the log bridge across the Bering
burst with a roar around
me again nothing but water,
brown water —
                    "Why not?"

FOR ROBERT KENNEDY

There are public men
become large as mountains or the endless forests
in the love men bear them
and when they die it is as if a great emptiness became
solid things turn misty and hard to hold onto
and the stunned heart clutches at dear remembrance
retraces its steps back somewhere in the past
when nothing changed and the high sun hangs motionless
friends remain fixed there and dogs bite gently
it is always morning it is always evening
                    it is always noon

And there are men newspapers never heard of
but loved for no reason or every reason
like my ugly grandfather who was

84

260 pounds of scarred lumberjack
hellraiser and backwoods farmer
of whom I said and say again
"— death takes him
as it takes more beautiful things
populations of whole countries
museums and works of art
and women with such a glow
            it makes their background vanish
they vanish too — "

But I'm wrong
one drives a beat-up Ford to find them
ten towns away across the belted planets
or waiting in the next apartment
one travels light
years across our heavy sorrow
to find the one man one man
and then another yet another
in the alchemy that changes
men but keeps them changeless
and solves the insoluble enigma
of blackjack death and the day's brief tenure
or fails perhaps
and becomes a genetic awareness
an added detail floating outward
inside the collective mind of humanity

THE HUNTING CAMP

Lost and wandering in circles
the camp seen for a third time
was like stubbing your toe
on a corpse

mouldy rotten logs an open grave
but the woods myth of continual circling
comfortingly verified as accurate
seemed a remote contact with warm human wisdom
It also seemed natural to address the trees
as a people substitute
but they would not speak
made no reply to his whispering yells
altho some were fat or thin
a few even looked a little friendly
but he told himself they were only trees
and said to them "You're only trees"
unsettled to hear himself
talking to a forest
That last time he saw the hunting camp
spectral with decay among the green life
something seemed to delay his own continuance
assuming continuance to be the sequence of thought
at least there was a gap in his life
he couldn't explain until afterwards
his last memory standing at an open tomb
which must have been the camp — then nothing
Afterwards
new-arriving bruises were evidence
of a few seconds when his brain had stopped
but feet had carried his mindless body forward
the forgotten feet slammed against trees
forest undergrowth whipped against his face
the feet bounced a body from tree to tree
and someone who was not his someone
had lived in his body during his death
then he re-occupied but without memory
only pain-evidence and a feeling of violation
his own thoughts beginning again and searching
for the stranger in his sixteen-year-old skull
In Hawk Junction distant as the moon

but only five miles away
he heard the trains' bodies shunting together
puzzled that sound came in waves and eddies
zig-zag voices that weren't there surrounding him
quite different from leaves touching other leaves
among which if you listened long enough
you might distinguish vegetable words
and he said to the leaves "What are you saying?"
In a clearing unaware of the sun
he might have seen a hairy man with humped shoulders
passing by intent on his own purposes
and wondered whether to ask directions
and wondered if he was capable of knowing
whether the thing was man or a bear
and felt pleasure at this intuition of instability
comforting as a pledge of fear of fear
Whatever time was went by
contracted or expanded somewhere in his skull
one thought went out to explore the brain's territory
among locked doors and doors slightly ajar
he kept arriving at blind alleys and places of no intention
— a second thought said trees had stopped speaking
a sub-thought said the trees had never spoken
but his thought consensus said they would someday
even tho trees were fat or thin but not human
trains actually were the hoarse voice of reality
Cooling sweat streaked his face and it pleased him
and the word for it pleased him: anodyne
which means release and solace from terror
he thought to make a song of it singing
and managing two syllables for every step
"O my darling O my darling Anodyne
You are lost and gone forever
dreadful sorry Anodyne"
and chuckled about the ridiculous sound
so exactly right for his regained calmness

then turning a street corner
in the forest found again
the hunting camp

Pre-School

Black was first of all
the place I came from
frightened because I couldn't remember
where I'd been or was going to
But when did I find yellow
in buttercup and dandelion
in the meadowlands and hill country
discover them in my mind
as if they had always been there
yellow eyes yellow eyes?
Red was about then too
and the river discovered me
lying upsidedown by the water
waiting for myself to happen
all the unfolding summer
while red willow roots waved
thru the water like a drowned girl's hair
I said as slowly as I could "You're red"
and it was so and I knew
I knew for the first time
that I could invent the world
Dark colours came later
of course after the blue sky
brown takes study to like much
tho some of the brown kind of people
have silver lights in their eyes
from the time the moon left here
because of a solemn promise

it gave the sun earlier on
and the brown people wanted to stay
in that gleaming landscape
and waited too long to leave:
in their minds are not quite clear
they haven't dreamed their sleeping
why it was there were no shadows
in that country without colour
but silver silver silver

Later on
the house went smaller and smaller
and green moss grew on the shingles
and all vegetable things in red and yellow
flowed orange and gold into women
and the grey child
went searching for one more colour
beyond blue eyes and brown hair
past the red tremble of leaves in October
and the silver women
beyond the death-black forest
to where all colours begin

ALIVE OR NOT

It's like a story
because it takes so long to happen:

a block away on an Ottawa street
I see this woman about to fall
and she collapses slowly
in sections the way you read about
and there just might be time
for me to reach her

running as fast as I can
before her head hits the sidewalk
Of course it's my wife
I am running toward her now
and there is a certain amount of horror
a time lag in which other things happen
I can almost see flowers break into blossom
while I am running toward the woman
my wife it seems
orchids in the Brazilian jungle
exist like unprovable ideas
until a man in a pith helmet
steps on one and yells Eureka or something
 — and while I am thinking about this
her body splashes on the street
her glasses fall broken beside her
with a musical sound under the traffic
and she is probably dead too
Of course I cradle her in my arms
a doll perhaps without life
while someone I do not know
signals a taxi
as the bystanders stare
What this means years later
as I grow older and older
is that I am still running toward her:
the woman falls very slowly
she is giving me more and more time
to reach her and make the grab
and each time each fall she may die
or not die and this will go on forever
this will go on forever and ever
As I grow older and older
my speed afoot increases
each time I am running and reach
the place before she falls every time

I am running too fast to stop
I run past her farther and farther
it's almost like a story
as an orchid dies in the Brazilian jungle
and there is a certain amount of horror

INSIDE THE MILL

It's a building where men are still working
thru sunlight and starlight and moonlight
despite the black holes plunging down
on their way to the roots of the earth
no danger exists for them
transparent as shadows they labour
in their manufacture of light

I've gone there lonely sometimes
the way I felt as a boy
and something lightened inside me
— old hands sift the dust that was flour
and the lumbering wagons returning
afloat in their pillar of shadows
as the great wheel turns the world

When you cross the doorway you feel them
when you cross the places they've been
there's a flutter of time in your heartbeat
of time going backward and forward
if you feel it and perhaps you don't
but it's voyaging backward and forward
on a gate in the sea of your mind

When the mill was torn down I went back there
birds fumed into fire at the place
a red sun beat hot in the stillness
they moved there transparent as morning

91

one illusion balanced another
as the dream holds the real in proportion
and the howl in our hearts to a sigh

THE DEATH MASK
(dated before 1200 BC, therefore too early to be Agamemnon's)

Thin gold pressed against a dead man's face
the tangible
          shaped by shadows
of the intangible and an error
on the draughting board of God
(some god or other)
transferred to a mask
The look of death that is a metal look
where the lines of a smile
of fear that began in life continue
changed into death's unindifference
for the double axe again poised
over scented bathwater and the Furies
gurgling down the drain
If death is like to death it is the bored face
that thrilled to other deaths
the going forth the not returning
and tall grass growing high on other streets
where others walk and meet and gossip
that now are goat-paths on a day
in Athens when the rain-dark hurrying clouds
that drown Apollo in their ragged hearts
and skirt museum walls but can't
douse the red flames of Troy
alight across the face of gold

Athens

A HANDFUL OF EARTH

to René Lévesque

Proposal:
let us join Quebec
if Quebec won't join us
I don't mind in the least
being governed from Quebec City
by Canadiens instead of Canadians
in fact the fleur-de-lis
                    and maple leaf
are only symbols
and our true language
speaks from inside
the land itself

Listen:
you can hear soft wind blowing
among tall fir trees on Vancouver Island
it is the same wind we knew
whispering along Côte des Neiges
on the island of Montreal
when we were lovers and had no money
Once flying in a little Cessna 180
above that great spine of mountains
where a continent attempts the sky
I wondered who owns this land
and knew that no one does
for we are tenants only

Go back a little:
to hip-roofed houses on the Isle d'Orléans
and scattered along the road to Chicoutimi
the remaining few log houses in Ontario
sod huts of sunlit prairie places
dissolved in rain long since

the stones we laid atop of one another
a few of which still stand
those origins
in which children were born
in which we loved and hated
in which we built a place to stand on
and now must tear it down?
— and here I ask all the oldest questions
of myself
the reasons for being alive
the way to spend this gift and thank the giver
but there is no way

I think of the small dapper man
chain-smoking at PQ headquarters
Lévesque
on Avenue Christophe Colomb in Montreal
where we drank coffee together six years past
I say to him now: my place is here
whether Côte des Neiges Avenue Christophe Colomb
Yonge Street Toronto Halifax or Vancouver
this place is where I stand
where all my mistakes were made
when I grew awkwardly and knew what I was
and that is Canadian or Canadien
it doesn't matter which to me

Sod huts break the prairie skyline
then melt in rain
the hip-roofed houses of New France as well
but French no longer
nor are we any longer English
— limestone houses
lean-tos and sheds our fathers built
in which our mothers died
before the forests tumbled down

ghost habitations
only this handful of earth
for a time at least
I have no other place to go

PRINCE EDWARD COUNTY

Words do have smell and taste
these have the taste of apples
brown earth and red tomatoes
as if a juggler had juggled
too many balls of fire
and dropped some of them
a smell and taste and bell sound
in the ear of waves
— not princes

Conservative since the Romans
— altho it's only animals
that are true conservatives
using the same land and water
and air for countless generations
themselves their own ancestors
each their own child
rabbits and groundhog tenants
porcupine leaseholders
and the wide estates of foxes

This is an island and you know
it's like being dressed in lace
as only a woman may be
and not be laughed at
around her neck and throat
the silver dance of coastlines
and bells rung deep in limestone

Animals having no human speech
have not provided names
but named it with their bodies
and the long-ago pine forests
named it with their bodies
and the masts of sailing ships
around the century's turn
named it to the sea
and a bird one springtime
named it bobolink bobolink
even a small unremarkable flower
I saw last April blossoming
that died shortly after
named it for herself
trillium

And we — the late-comers
white skins and brown men
no voice told us to stay
but we did for a lifetime
of now and then forever
the fox and flower and rabbit
and bells rung deep in limestone
— for any who come after
you have heard our names
and the word we made of silence
bobolink and —

Journey to the Sea

Zig-zag on the switchback road
over mountain country
in alpine clarity
trees have eaten their shadows
and many-fingered cactus
stand like prophets
pointing in all directions
to the Promised Land
Then down to the tropics
in sweatbox heat
and comet-blossoms of flowers
the yellow torch of primavera
a blue one for jacaranda
tents of blue-yellow
as the man-beetle floats down
— floats heavily down
with a pig-squeal of tires
Then a road not on maps
still being built
by prehistoric engineers
I daydream in the heat
of seeing a man waving
a red flag on the road
shouting Turn Back Turn Back
We slosh and dribble
thru thin brown rivers
near half-built bridges
and overturned wheelbarrows
— a crashed airplane at roadside
mashed aluminum bug
the pilot certainly dead
and thinking: how awful to die
reeling down from up there
allotting yourself just seconds

to remember the best things
counting from one to twenty
— eight my love and six my love
and three for yellow primavera
and then forgetting
Washouts and stone slides
where the mountain spared us
by acting a moment before
we came or a moment after
At the world's last corner
a mountain shelf
maybe a thousand feet high
and nothing but space
an empty blue room
— and if there was anywhere
a First Cause
it had hidden itself perfectly
by remaining in plain sight
without intention or design
blue robes and blue sandals
spread out before us
like the altar cloths of heaven
an aching majesty of nothing
while we drink beer

Mexico

∿

MAY 23, 1980

I'd been driving all day
arrived home around 6 p.m.
got something to eat and slept an hour
then I went outside
and you know

— the whole world smells of lilacs
the whole damn world

I have grown old
making lists of things I wanted
to do and other lists
of words I wanted to say
and laughed because of the lists
and forgot most of them
— but there was a time
and there was this girl
this girl with violet eyes
and a lot of other people too
because it was some kind of a party
— but I couldn't think of a way
some immediate plan or method
to bathe in that violet glow
with a feeling of being there too
at the first morning of the world
So I jostled her elbow a little
spilled her drink all over
did it again a couple of times
and you know it worked
it got so she winced
every time she saw me coming
but I did get to talk to her
and she smiled reluctantly
a little cautious because
on the basis of observed behaviour
I might be mad
and then she smiled
— altho I've forgotten her name
it's on one of those lists

I have grown old
but these words remain

tell her for me
because it's very important
tell her for me
there will come one May night
of every year that she's alive
when the whole world smells of lilacs

RED FOX ON HIGHWAY 500
(near midnight)

All I saw was the tail of him
the dream fox ahead of me
his rump a red light flashing
in a thousand movie still shots
(callipygous screenland special)
forty feet ahead of me
feet red hammers hammering
light as air on the highway
running from death on the highway
he died or dreamed he did
— his tail a flat red poker
flung straight back toward me
his eyes overtaking his shadow
his tail bisecting the moonlight
he was fox fox fox

It was like a stage play
it was like my childhood nightmares
the guilt-ridden dreams of running
when all the adults chased me
but nobody ever caught me
it was like time had stopped for us
and never begins again
His shadow black as a monster

100

his shadow a soundless monster
stomping the dark ahead of us
suffering when we suffer
dying when we die

And I saw us running
I watched us doing it
the car the fox the shadow
those other selves for witness
— and I wondered about things
I wondered about all sorts of things
his face and what he looked like
apart from a million foxes
the rest of his breed and kin
and whether his foxy character
glowed in his brain and eye
about this damn predicament
of having a dozen bodies
like fascinated observers
all of them watching us watching
deep in the moonlight forest
or under the bedclothes loving
or killing another animal
I was really philosophical
it was almost like a poem
and it had to end precisely
at ten minutes after midnight
so that I could drive to Belleville
keep an appointment in Belleville
and never forget a word

So here we are
and here we have been forever
running and running and running
your mate in the nearby forest
wondering where you got to

and failed to keep your appointment
an hour ago in the cedars
the mystery of why things happen
this way and never that way
the reason you kept her waiting
an hour or was it your lifetime
in case you go under the wheels

Of course I stopped
and gates of the moonlight opened
and lightly he stepped inside
— it was silent that kind of silence
when live events are waiting
jammed at the doors of time
frozen in silver moonlight
then leaped into flux again
— he had to keep his appointment
no matter how late it was
and I had to drive to Belleville
both of us had our plans
plans of the utmost importance
for going on living longer
for eating and drinking and sleeping
and maybe loving someone
for killing other animals
for being noble and human
or fox fox fox

SHOT GLASS MADE FROM A BULL'S HORN
(once owned by Ralph Purdy)

A young ensign set lips to this cup.
I drink from it now. In 1815,
one Francis Gore, Lieutenant-gov.
of Upper Can., gave him his commish.
The cup is dark brown with gold lights.
It's attractive to me for such reasons,
with initials R.P. deeply incised,
and a crude Brit. flag cut in bone.
I presume R.P. was my ancestor,
when George something-or-other was king,
at a time when the French Rev. was
alarming grocers: Ralph went swaggering
into a pub full of joy in himself,
and talked nonsense in some girl's ear:
after the fiasco of 1812,
love was the thing and war a bore.
Here's to you Ralph with good rye,
when kings are quaint and Canada is
a country ending at the beginning,
but love and sex continue thru history:
somewhere a phantom ensign is waving his sword,
and somewhere his backwoods Jerusalem survives:
wholly ridiculous and quite unreal,
where the great trees stand and a stone sun
glares down on settlers in the remote forest:
a mythic country that disbelieves in itself,
but whose citizens yet declare allegiance,
and still feel mortal love and hurtful pain,
and drink to both from a bull's horn . . .

Bestiary

Burro sounds
in early morning
six eight ten syllables of a rusty iron gate
squeaking open and closed
the long guttural word of speaking
that hears itself from outside the burro's body
earth-wail of the burro-soul
and hairy old man's ears lift listening
unheavenly jewsharpgutstretchingmouthfartingmusic
stymies sleep
touching the far rim of being
the solemn lost edge of things
when the first cry was a new thing
that said this is who I am
and to hell with mountains

Mourning doves
roosting in eucalyptus trees
above flaming poinsettia
a throaty non-bird sound
gurgling insomniac sound
that goes whispering back and twists
itself into serpent hiss
old father of lies on his crawling belly
reptilian ancestor without song
goes slumbering back to the great lizards
kin to the lizard
chickadee chirp
in a snake's mouth

Rooster boast
two short and one long syllable
sends blood plummeting skyward
where he can no longer go
and declares in rooster
earth is best earth is best
and heart knows that isn't true

the brag-song is a grief-cry
earth at best is second-best
he mourns the sky the lost sky
with a metal windvane rooster
dodging lightning atop a northern barn
he is sky-lost
the white stovelid a lost glory
poor flightless bird

Dogs
barking and threatening
harassing each other
then into the mob-gabble and out
again emerges one long wavering howl
so close to the man-howl in extremis
self-pitying man-cry
all is lost all is lost
then moving along the scale down down
the dog-soul plaintive and wavering
saying piteously
I am so lonely so one-single
I have so much personality
such tragic grandeur
then frightening himself into seriousness
a disembodied ghost-voice trembling
among red pomegranate and mango trees
calling Father Dog and Grandfather Wolf
all the way back to the Cambrian
and Precambrian when there were no wolves
no housepets
only the still cooling world
earth steaming and boiling
in the ovens of creation

Mexico

105

In the Garden

Poinsettias blaze red bougainvillaeas burn
the lake is a smooth blue plate
for sun-tongues to lick clean
Once maybe at the very beginning of things
everything was mud-coloured
you could look out and see only grey sand
you could see nothing to send messages
back from it to you
just dirty-coloured seawater
where rain had lashed things in fury
and wind mixed everything up like soft porridge
and only the pole-star shone like a white lever
for gods of the sky to shinny down
on long slender columns of light
and arrive on earth with a cry
Then we had blue and scarlet and silver
then we had vegetable love
whoever was looking for something
dreamed it first of all
then we made a wanting song of sadness
then we made a finding song of joy
when the Moon said "Here I am Sun"
so he was
and went on sailing up there
all night for the first time

It must have been if you were watching
if you could have watched in the morning
a time to stand naked in rain
a time to feel the fingers of warm rain
touching your new human body
and stammer some praise for it
          your thanks — and you had to thank someone
why not the earth?

Thank you earth thank you sea thank you sky
the beginnings of human love
when we said:
                    these things are dear
they are bought with your life
they are yours for only an instant
they are yours unconditionally
then you must give them away

Mexico

MOONSPELL

I have forgotten English
in order to talk to pelicans
plunging into tomorrow
disturb the deep reverie
of herons standing
on yesterday's shoreline
find the iguana's secret
name embroidered
on his ruby brain
it is milk
it is moonlight
milk pouring
over the islands
stand in a doorway
listen
I am drowning
in sky milk
and those soft murmurings
of moonlit vertebrae
these deciphered codewords
are spoken names

of island dwellers
they will not be repeated
pour on my bare shoulders
are small extensions
of themselves
as the manta ray bubbles
rising in water
gleams in moonlight
small fish tremble
I know I know
my speech is grunts
squeaks clicks stammers
let go let go
follow the sunken ships
and deep sea creatures
follow the *protozoa*
into that far darkness
another kind of light
leave off this flesh
this voice
these bones
sink down

Galapagos Islands

BIRDWATCHING AT THE EQUATOR

The blue-footed booby
stands on her tropic island
in the Galapagos group
stands all day long
shading her eggs from the sun
also protecting her blue feet
from too much ultraviolet

Sometimes the male booby
flaps his wings and dances
to entertain his mate
pointing his toes upward
so they can discuss blueness
which seems to them very beautiful
Their only real enemy
is the piratical frigate bird
floating on great black wings
above the mile-long island
Sometimes the frigate bird
robs them of their fish
whereupon the booby
is wont to say "Friggit"
and catches some more
When night comes all the boobies
sit down at once as if
God had given them a signal
or else one booby says
to the rest "Let's flop boys"
and they do

The blue booby's own capsule
comment about evolution:
if God won't do it for you
do it yourself:
stand up
sit down
make love
have some babies
catch fish
dance sometimes
admire your feet
friggit:
what else is there?

Galapagos Islands

PILING BLOOD

It was powdered blood
in heavy brown paper bags
supposed to be strong enough
to prevent the stuff from escaping
but didn't

We piled it ten feet high
right to the shed roof
working at Arrow Transfer
on Granville Island
The bags weighed 75 pounds
and you had to stand on two
of the bags to pile the top rows
I was six feet three inches
and needed all of it

I forgot to say
the blood was cattle blood
horses sheep and cows
to be used for fertilizer
the foreman said

It was a matter of some delicacy
to plop the bags down softly
as if you were piling dynamite
if you weren't gentle
the stuff would belly out
from bags in brown clouds
settle on your sweating face
cover hands and arms
enter ears and nose
seep inside pants and shirt
reverting back to liquid blood
and you looked like

you'd been scalped
by a tribe of
particularly unfriendly
Indians and forgot to die

We piled glass as well
it came in wooden crates
two of us hoicking them
off trucks into warehouses
every crate
weighing 200 pounds
By late afternoon
my muscles would twitch and throb
in a death-like rhythm
from hundreds of bags of blood
and hundreds of crates of glass

Then at Burns' slaughterhouse
on East Hastings Street
I got a job part time
shouldering sides of frozen beef
hoisting it from steel hooks
staggering to and from
the refrigerated trucks
and eerie freezing rooms
with breath a white vapour
among the dangling corpses
and the sound of bawling animals
screeched down from an upper floor
with their throats cut
and blood gurgling into special drains
for later retrieval

And the blood smell clung to me
clung to clothes and body
sickly and sweet

and I heard the screams of dying cattle
and I wrote no poems
there were no poems
to exclude the screams
which boarded the streetcar
and travelled with me
till I reached home
turned on the record player
and faintly
in the last century
heard Beethoven weeping

GONDWANALAND

*(Some 200 million years ago — according to geological theory —
there was only one landmass on earth, the supercontinent called
Pangaea, meaning "single land." Then a large chunk broke away
from Pangaea; it has been named Gondwanaland. The new
Gondwanaland split up and drifted south and west to become
Africa, Australia and South America. The remaining continent, now
called Laurasia, also broke apart, some of it drifting west to become
North America, the remainder Europe and Asia.)*

The planet's basic stone
and what they did with it
those old ones:
— stone as art forms
shaped rearranged caressed worshipped
unknown men hammering stone on stone
common stuff from deep within
                        earth's mantle
at Machu Picchu Sacsahuayman Carnac
artisans of the finite

Earlier still
stone islands grating against stone islands
(Gondwanaland dear lost Gondwanaland
and the worm's birthplace Pangaea
when one world self became many
and earth said to earth Goodbye)
when the birds the coloured birds
cried in their sleep for home
and dinosaurs riding stone galleons westward
an inch a year for centuries
lived and died like sailors

And stone as exterior decoration
sliced naked thru road cuts
of the Appalachians
and Precambrian Shield
grey oatmeal-porridge stuff
criss-cross tweedy patterns
stone like pink cooked ham
— or diamond speckled bits of light
twinkling on a party dress
across the millennia
in a bring-the-jubilee summons
to a five-billion-year-old
birthday on a one-room planet

(and perhaps two lovers —
their identity doesn't matter
— but maybe you and I are
those puppets caught up
in earth's divine passion
or mere human rut
hands linked in consecration
eyes trustful of each other
that the spell will last forever
— we join the celebration

while time performs its wonders
its carbon miracles)

Sedimentary rock
where a fallen leaf
prints itself on stone
and dies forever
Organic limestone
when skeletons of marine creatures
drifted down floating down in green gloom
each one turning a little in the water
and seeming to nod to each other
as they passed by
until their bones jostled in tiny mimic strugglings
with other bones at the misty graveyard
on the sea bottom

And fossil stone
in which mineral salts
have replaced animal bones:
far in the future a crew of
skeletons replacing living men
under earth's dying sun
crews of fossil mariners
riding ships of floating stone
without meaning or purpose
for there was never any purpose
and there was never any meaning —

Only that we listened to the birds
or saw how the sun coloured the sky
and were thoughtful in quiet moments
Sometimes in these short lives
when our minds drifted off alone
moving in the space vacated by leaves
to allow sunlight to pass thru

at the wind's soft prompting
there was reasonable content
that we were aware of only afterwards
and clapping our hands together like children
we broke the spell

Cairn on an arctic island
blind shape turned seaward
what sails rise there?

IN THE BEGINNING WAS THE WORD

In the Beginning was not *the Word*
— but a Chirrup.

        D.H. Lawrence

We made our speech from moving water
a sound that seems to ache
when there is no pain
whispering faintly in the heart's darkness
— and listening at still pools in the forest
we saw the strangers and fled in fear
from their floating faces
We made our speech from the wind's voice
singing to earth when the moon sleeps
and in weariness after hunting
the red throat of fire the white tongues of rain
We made it from the sound of food
on little pattering feet running
with terrified eyes in the forest
while we watched in ambush
with wet mouths
We made our speech from all things
weaker than us and the sounds moved
when our tongues moved

as if they were alive and they were alive
and our children played with the sounds
until they remembered silence

We made our speech from the beast's growl
the bird's chirp and dumb thunder muttering
and from the ice-spirit at the glacier's edge
desolate voices of the lost ones calling
And we changed the colours of things
into sounds of themselves
for we were the great imitators
and we spoke the strong words that invented men
and became ourselves
And we painted our dead crimson
in order that the blood should remember
in all their voyaging the place they came from

And after the essence of everything
had exchanged itself for words and became
another being and could even be summoned
from far distance we chanted a spell of names
and we said "Mountain be our friend"
and we said "River guard us from enemies"
And we said what it seemed the gods themselves
might say if we had dreamed them and they
had dreamed us from their high places
and they spoke to us in the forest
from the river and the mountain
and the mouths of the ochre-painted dead
had speech again and the waters
spoke and the silence had words

And our children remembered —

Adam and no Eve

His name is *Geochelone (elephantopus) abingdoni*
a giant yellow-faced tortoise
the last of his species
(call him Lonesome George)
from Abingdon Island
now coddled and cuddled by keepers
the nursemaid scientists
of Darwin Research Station

They have posted reward money
these scientists
ten thousand dollars
for just one female
of Lonesome George's species
but no female has ever been found
Lonesome George's relatives
brothers and sisters and cousins
stern great aunts and harrumphing uncles
are gone from Abingdon Island
and the world

(Summon the bounty hunters:
is there movement somewhere
among the man-high cactus
with four legs instead of two
and neck like a periscope
wandering the 20th century?
— a clumsy shadow blunders
through laboratory glassware
could that be Great Aunt Martha?
— a sudden splash of light
along the mangrove shoreline
could that be Abingdon Annie?)

Man with his symbol-making brain
has said ten thousand dollars
equals one female
but there are millions and billions
of dollars in pockets and banks
and no tortoises in their vaults
or human pockets and wallets
— in fact make it a billion
dollars for one nubile female
the result is exactly the same

Not again shall mud conceive
or the stars bear witness
and lightning flash over chaos
nor any deity of the flesh
send his small amphibians
scuttling onto land for safety
the amino acids are dissolved
their formulas forgotten
— and whatever love may be
weighed and counted and measured
in books and artistic symbols
one female tortoise (shaped
somewhat like an old shoe)
has taken it with her alone
into the darkness

Galapagos Islands

IN THE EARLY CRETACEOUS

They came overnight
a hundred million years ago
the first flowers ever

a new thing under the sun
invented by plants
It must have been around 7 a.m.
when a shrew-like mammal stumbled
out of its dark burrow
and peered nearsightedly
at the first flower with
an expression close to amazement
and decided it wasn't dangerous

In the first few centuries later
flowers began to cover the earth
in springtime they glowed
with gleaming iridescence
not just a tiny bouquet
like the colours on a mallard's neck
before mallards existed
or like god's earmuffs
before Genesis was written
and even tho nobody was there
to analyze it
they nevertheless produced a feeling
you couldn't put a name to
which you could only share
like moonlight on running water
        leaf-talk in the forest
the best things right under your nose
and belonging to everyone

And one of the early inhabitants
a comic-looking duck-billed dinosaur
might have lifted his head
with mouth full of dripping herbage
and muttered Great Scott
or something like it
Triceratops gulped a township
of yellow blossoms
diplodocus sampled blue

for several horizons
and thought it was heavenly
and colour became food

It was not a motionless glory
for colours leaped off the earth
they glowed in the sky
when wind blew great yellow fields
danced undulating in sunlight
hundreds of miles of blue flowers
were dark velvet in starlight
and maybe some unnamed creature
stayed awake all night in the
midst of a thousand miles of colour
just to see what it felt like
to have all the blue-purple there was
explode in his brain
and alter both present and future

But no one will ever know
what it was like
that first time on primordial earth
when bees went mad with pollen fever
and seeds flew away from home
on little drifting white parachutes
without a word to their parents
— no one can ever know
even when someone is given
the gift of a single rose
and behind that one rose
are the ancestors of all roses
and all flowers and all the springtimes
for a hundred million years
of summer and for a moment
in her eyes an echo
of the first tenderness

MUSEUM PIECE

This boneyard of the dinosaurs
finds me footsore and tired
of all fleamarket history
that sets such store on paperclips
the toilet bric-a-brac of queens
their bowel movements chronicled
by scared astrologers
But ah the dinosaurs they soar
to fifteen twenty thirty metres
(or Biblical cubits if you prefer):
their body sounds of gurglings
rumblings of ancient indigestion
monstrous mooing love complaints
sunk to soft earthworm murmurs

Stand under these bone shadows
of tons of onetime flesh
and the mind harks back
to their heyday in the late
Cretaceous when the Great Death
came and saith: — "All life is mine"
— the red sun stopped its seeming flight
the planet's moon returned to night
when the shapeless shape no man hath seen
walked abroad in its shroud
and Eden gates went clang
shut with no sound

But ah they soared they Soar
this walled space makes no mock
of those with such enormous
appetites they ate the world
When museum cleaners come here
and leave aside their mops and brooms

to climb up teetery stepladders
with rags to wipe the weeklong dust
from fossil craniums they must
tremble a little no matter what
accident insurance rates are
The mind shuffles its feet to think
of that time: — when diplodocus tyrannosaurus
and the like trumpeted at the sky
65 million years ago
and it occurs to me that our human ancestors
then were small shrew-like creatures
hiding in holes probably nocturnal
— in that instant notice the cleaners
atop their stepladders have all changed
back into small shrew-like creatures
with tragic eyes

VOLTAIRE

Travelling home to Cirey
with Madame du Châtelet
over the frozen roads of Europe
at night in March 1737:
a wheel came off the carriage
on Voltaire's side and it turned over
piling everything — baggage
the "divine Émilie" and her maid
atop Voltaire with considerable
objection from the great man
— at the same time the two drivers
tumbled headfirst down the roadway
inventing some new cusswords
and horses haunted by ghosts of predators
stampeded inside their harness

When Voltaire was extricated
and servants worked to restore order
quieting the nervous horses
he began to enjoy himself
Cushions were laid on the winter road
Voltaire and his mistress sat on them
laughing together about the accident
until the carriage was repaired
and appreciating the night sky
One of the servants describes it:
"Not a tree, not a house
disturbed the expanse of the horizon.
M. de Voltaire and Madame
du Châtelet were in ecstasies:
wrapped in furs, they discussed
the nature and orbits of the stars
and their destination in space,
while their teeth chattered.
If only they had had a telescope,
their joy would have been complete."

All over Europe
generals marched their armies
the Inquisition tortured heretics
kings sat uneasily on their thrones
sniffing the wine suspiciously
and babies were waiting to be born
while "divine Émilie" and her lover
laughed on the frozen roads of France

Something ridiculous about it
Voltaire and Émilie on that frozen road
like strange children
with their grown-up servants
— you can peer inside their heads
see the litter of toys and games

among the measuring devices of science
and think "Genius is children"
it lives in far Centaurus
and star clusters beyond cold Orion
and sometimes visits earth
when there is no one home

~~

ELEGY FOR A GRANDFATHER

Well, he died, I guess. They said he did.
His wide whalebone hips will make a prehistoric barrow
men of the future may find and marvel on:
where this man's relatives ducked their heads
in real and pretended sorrow
for the dearly beloved gone thank Christ to God
after a bad century, a tough big-bellied Pharaoh,
with a deck of cards in his pocket and a Presbyterian grin —

Maybe he did die, but the boy didn't understand it;
the man knows now and the scandal never grows old
of a happy lumberjack who lived on rotten whiskey,
and died of sin and Quaker oats age 90 or so.
But all he was was too much for any man to be,
a life so full he couldn't include one more thing,
nor tell the same story twice if he'd wanted to,
and didn't and didn't —

Just the same he's dead. A sticky religious voice
folded his century sideways to get it out of sight,
and lowered him into the ground like someone still alive
who had to be handled very carefully,
even after death he made people nervous:
and earth takes him as it takes more beautiful things:
populations of whole countries,

museums and works of art,
and women with such a glow
it makes their background vanish
                              they vanish too
and Lesbos' singer in her sunny islands
stopped when the sun went down —

No, my grandfather was decidedly unbeautiful,
260 pounds of scarred slag,
barnraiser and backwoods farmer,
poker player and brawling lumberjack:
become an old man in a one-room apartment
over a drygoods store,
become anonymous as a dead animal
whose chemicals may not be reconstituted.
There is little doubt that I am the sole
repository of his remains: which consist of
these flashing pictures in my mind,
which I can't bequeath to anyone,
which stop here: juice and flavour
of the old ones, whose blood runs thin
in mine: mustard, cayenne, ammonia,
brimstone (trace only above his grave)
                              — a dying soup-stained giant
who scared hell outa me sometimes
other times I listen fascinated
overhearing him curse God in my own arteries —

Which is a bit too romantic
— say again what he was:
parrot beak and watery blue
eyes that stared at you
like piss-holes in the snow
and around him
people grew serious
without ever knowing why
you stopped feeling clever

and shuffled your feet
uncomfortably
aware you were being judged
by other standards
than your mother's
and yet I loved him
with no explanation for it:
he didn't echo your own feelings
and aim them back at you
he didn't grin mindlessly
he was what the words said
and perhaps above all
he was not a copy of anything
he reminded you of nothing but himself
and frighteningly
I think it very probable
there are other descendants
besides myself
but with different surnames
than my own
(knowing his propensities)
maybe a few
with that parrot beak
watery blue eyes
and not very loveable
— on streets and rivers and mountains
at meetings anywhere
I will know them

1956–1986–1996

THE SMELL OF ROTTEN EGGS

The cancer had taken both breasts
and I got the strange impression
that what was left of her
was not really sentient
and wherever cancerous breasts get thrown
two of them mourned their lost body

One almost expected to see
death actually arrive
dressed in sombre medieval garb
or cap and bells like the king's fool
dancing and capering
But there is nothing in books
to match this savagery
the scene in which we are both audience
and players dredged up from a child's
nightmares to achieve instant reality:
on the leading actor's face the clenched rictus
of a slightly amused grin

(You cannot find anything here
in your mind or the hospital room
to make things less unpleasant for you
and must retreat into total selfishness
to avoid suddenly seeing yourself in bed
with the woman's corpse and fucking it)

A survivor of World War I
once told me that before mustard gas
attacks and the creeping yellow clouds
joined you in muddy trenches
there was always the odour of rotten eggs
and death was made smellable
before you soaked a handkerchief in piss

and clapped it over your nose
if you didn't have a gas mask
And I smell death in this cancerous room
and clap both hands over my mouth
and start running

I have always tried to avoid unpleasant things
bad smells — death — physical pain
and never been able to
flowers stink beauty rots gods die
we can hardly seize one good instant
of sunlight for ourselves and hold onto it
in our minds before it turns monster
It is no panacea
to describe these various aspects of horror
and no help to name the names of things
nevertheless I name names

THE PRISON LINES AT LENINGRAD
for Anna Akhmatova

She speaks for them
            — the speechless dead:
the woman in her chill misery
who said, "Could you describe this?"
Akhmatova answering, "Yes."

They led her husband off like a dog,
already emptiness in his heart
— in hers the poems since, a song
that echoes in soundless prison yards.

Number 300 — is she still here,
mourning husband, mourning child?

— the Neva's ice-choked water spares
no swimmer, cannot hear their cries.

The Peterhof in Baltic mist,
and Peter's statue in greenish bronze;
Stalin inside the Kremlin walls
drills unhearing firing squads.

The Tsars arise to cheer themselves,
that's Nicholas who used to wet the bed;
and hand on hip, standing negligently,
a man with ice pick in his head.

Siberia — the name like an anthem,
is requiem for millions dead;
no Mozart here with his last breath
to choir an immense Russian sadness . . .

"Far from your ocean, Leningrad,
I leave my body" — they heard the cry,
those prisoners, their anthem hers:
the dead earth becomes alive.

～⌒

QUETZAL BIRDS

They exist somewhere between yes and no
that three-foot tail has elements of both
I have not really seen green till now
sea-leaf-emerald dire-jade-jealousy green
so imploded and concentrated one hears
it chunking at the soul's rear window

Only chiefs might wear those tail feathers
not dukes duchesses belted earls

                    just Kings
— in another life on the hot dry plains of Anahuac
I have seen thousands waiting — the commoners
Aztec Mixtec Toltec Mayan unemotional
unquestioning yearning they-know-not-what
faces like scabbards of swords

I knew a guy once would buy a single drop
of perfume worth a trillion bucks
for a girl he knew on the next block
— the quetzal is like that
one glimpse
dipping above the well at Chichen Itza
skimming the sorrowful deserts of Yucatan
and troubled haciendas of Guatemala
this non-Christian-Muslim atheist deity
squeezes the heart

                ~~~

THE OTHERS

                    I

We are not alone in the world
our brothers the animals
                our sisters the birds
— at the making day they were late
and the creatures of sea and marsh
remained when We crawled away

With the host on the salt plain's edge
at the giving out of hands
they were chasing each other's tails
or sniffing each other's ass
— when the maker of land and sea
questioned about their souls

there was howling among the trees

When they handed out the blessings
and looked deep in their creatures' eyes
they responded with great unease
and could not meet that gaze

At the naming of things We know
they chirped and hissed and growled
and went with the winds of the world
— when they died their scattered bones
were forbidden the Holy Ground

Ignorant of what they are not
unaware of things that they are
their memory is lost as Eden
their anger the same as fear

II

To follow a trail through the forest
and not think
                    "Have I been here before?"
or remember an odd-shaped stone
that hitch-hiked to now with a glacier
from the last Ice Age
a stone reminding them of something else
and triggered a whole series of rememberings
or notice a daisy like the day's eye
déjà vu in the etymological dark
— but how do we *know* that?
Perhaps the caribou with antler antennae
in their hundreds of thousands
have stood on some primordial beach
near Great Bear Lake listening
to music from the Crab Nebula
the debris of a supernova

in a caribou fantasy
— or the arctic wolf searching
his genes all the way back to Genesis
for the Godwolf's terrible face
— at least the deer's soft helpless look
facing death wraps up that moment
for the time when we die ourselves
and the far distant eye from nowhere
peers with instinctive distaste
into our own brief lives

IN THE DESERT
for Milton Acorn

My friends die off one by one:
and far away in the desert
caravans are plodding thru the sand
I can see them at the horizon's edge
the young on their many roads to Mecca
but I have been there often
and returned again

My friends die off:
far distant in waste places
the living move in many directions
I could run after them shouting
across the desert "Wait for me — "
And sometimes I have done that
but things went badly for me
and rushing to meet those people
excited and panting
their faces change into someone else
their faces change . . .

This morning
wandering the grey desert
looking for a cactus flower
in the wrong season
with caravans moving in the distance
sinking under grey horizons
I noticed someone moving in the shadows
coming toward me at a great pace
and they cried out as I had done
"Wait for me — "

A single figure
but impossible to say
whether it was male or female
crossing the sand dunes shouting
arriving where I stand waiting
in a great flurry of dust and sand:
it was someone I did not know
and very young
I was about to say in a neutral voice
"You had better go back — "

But looking into that eager face
and hopeful eyes — : I glimpsed the flux
of what exists and does not yet exist
a wavering between disappointment and joy
and knew there was only a moment left
before the little gap in time healed itself
I said welcome
and knew this messenger from the desert
was someone I had been waiting for
and clasped them in my arms
the stranger

ON THE FLOOD PLAIN

Midnight:
it's freezing on the lake
and wind whips ice eastward
but most of the water remains open
— and stars visit earth
tumbled about like floating candles
on the black tumulus
then wind extinguishes the silver fire
but more flash down
and even those reflections reflect
on the sides of waves
even the stars' reflections reflect stars

Ice:
far older than earth
primordial as the Big Bang
— cold unmeasured by Celsius and Fahrenheit
quarrelling about it on a Jurassic shingle
— before Pangaea and Gondwanaland
arrive here in the 20th century
born like a baby
under the flashlight beam
Bend down and examine the monster
and freeze for your pains
— tiny oblong crystals
seem to come from nowhere
little transparent piano keys
that go tinkle tinkle tinkle
while the wind screams
— and you feel like some shivering hey
presto god grumbling at his fucked-up weather
hurry indoors hurry indoors to heaven

People have told us we built too near the lake
"The flood plain is dangerous" they said
and no doubt they know more about it than we do
— but here wind pressed down on new-formed ice
trembles it like some just-invented musical instrument
and that shrieking obbligato to winter
sounds like the tension in a stretched worm
when the robin has it hauled halfway out of the lawn
I stand outside
between house and outhouse
feeling my body stiffen in fossilized rigor mortis
and listening
thinking
this is the reason we built on the flood plain
damn right
the seriousness of things beyond your understanding

Whatever I have not discovered and enjoyed
is still waiting for me
and there will be time
but now are these floating stars on the freezing lake
and music fills the darkness
holds me there listening
— it's a matter of separating these instants from others
that have no significance
so that they keep reflecting each other
a way to live and contain eternity
in which the moment is altered and expanded
my consciousness hung like a great silver metronome
suspended between stars
on the dark lake
and time pours itself into my cupped hands shimmering

Seasons

Winter
in our thoughts of each other
and I remember
the way another woman looked
at me as if I were the most
least thing on earth
and I was somehow I was
my own existence ended
and summer gradually coming on
to fill my vacuum in her mind
In late winter
before the melting time
the crocus stirred preparing
underground for its spring entrance
I lessened and grew more:
all least things affect me in season
all those remnants of memory
wind-worn and transparent
seen from the other side of now
as if I were looking at you
across some kind of curtain
and you were looking at me
from another curtain
as all things lessened
and grew more

Summer was very late that year
the birds seemed bewildered
questioning each other about snow
which some had never seen before
ice rimed the shorelines
and made small tinkling sounds
as if to say welcome
but wind blew colder

and they sent messages
to relatives farther
south and said "Don't come"
It made no difference
the weasel's red eye glittered
foxes hunted and the human hunters
blew on their hands shivering
We shrugged close to the heater
and didn't speak
I would have said
"Why do you hate me?"
but it was useless
we grunted with our eyes

Let me be quite forgotten
and come to think of it
I want to be
anonymous as a raindrop
slightly off course and falling
away from the sun maybe
finding the slim wingbones
of a bird among the cedars
a bird who may have thought
"oh dear — oh dear — oh dear"
before dying
let me be quite forgotten
as snow falls from the red sun
like a thousand thousand flowers
until our tracks are covered

GLACIER SPELL

Ice — islands archipelagos continents
worlds of ice
stretching north and holding the sea prisoner
wriggling uneasily in the moon's hypnosis
— and meltwater drains at the glacier's south
where a smaller sea reflects its monster parent
east and west a blue witch-light
spreads into darkness
And year by year the ice recedes
an inch or a foot on the sun's yardstick
yielding entombed creatures thawing slowly
till ice unlocks them
and they tumble from the shoulder-breech
with earth regained they tremble and shudder
appear to take a step then sink to their knees
suffering a double life and a double death
while the ice rings with a dumb chanting

As the sun strengthens a slender line of green
paints itself crookedly at the glacier's foot
and plant faces turn away from the cold
— when rains come a hundred miles of ice
and a thousand miles of sky join in
the roar of drainage to a southbound river
a sound heard by no one
— only a wandering hunter
outcast from his tribe
a man with demons in his heart
unexpectedly not at home
in the great sky rooms of earth

Time speeds and slows
moves in the altering shape of stillness
speeding to plant a forest

slowing to welcome a bird
waiting for the first beast
while the glacier pretends it isn't there
but shitting lateral moraines
— a brown man and a brown woman
day eyes peering at night eyes
of animals outside
the fire's cave of red light
through the black and white door
where fear waits

Do not touch words to what has no name
or feel the place of wandering stones with eyes
the beast we hunt must not be said
its smell rides under the wind
its face remembers our faces

PROCNE INTO ROBIN

To dance like that in firelight
with music playing
and throw off all your clothes
around midnight
is no ordinary woman's way
with a man and no
you are no ordinary
woman but a bird
I have just made this discovery
— not the Greek bird Procne
                nor her sister Philomela
not swallow or nightingale
as the gods changed them to —
not exactly your namesake either
for she is much too red-breasted

and you're white all over or nearly
I have made another discovery
those short dainty steps of yours
are the shore-birds dance steps
on a storm-battered beach
after the rough waves recede
stitching the world back together
And when you hover over me
I am already at your feet
unable to say anything
only murmur as men do
and wait
when they know the little dancer
from the sky must rest sometimes
must rest soon
with folded wings
and wait

On Being Human

When my mother went to hospital
after a fall alone in her bedroom
I was eighteen miles away
trying to build a house

I visited her later
and something in my face made her say
"I thought you'd feel terrible"
and she meant that I'd be devastated
by what had happened to her
— I wasn't feeling anything very much
at the time and I guess it showed
just thinking I'd have to travel
those eighteen miles every day

to visit her and grumbling to myself
At that moment
she had seen behind the shutters
normally drawn across the human face
and suddenly realized
there wasn't much if any
affection for her in my face
and that knowledge
was worse than her injuries

But there is no going back in time
to do anything about it now
if something wasn't done then
and nothing was
She died not much later
her mind disoriented
forgetting what happened to her
but I remember those last words
list them first
among the things I'm ashamed of
as intolerable as realizing
your whole life has been wasted
— remembering my cousin's words
about her drunken brother:
"It would have been better
if he'd never lived at all"

I remember those last words
before the fever took her mind
and the only good thing now
is thinking about those words
and she is instantly
restored to life
in my mind
and repeats the same words
"I thought you'd feel terrible"

again and again and again
and I am still ashamed
and I am still alive

[Once, on Baffin Island,] I was curled up in a sleeping bag, feeling lost at the world's edge, bereft of family and friends. As the tide went out, icebergs were left stranded on the beach. With the water's support removed, they collapsed on themselves with a crash whose echoes kept repeating themselves. A dog would howl, and others join in, a bedlam chorus. Old Squaw ducks moaned about how awful life was, an *OUW-OUW-OUW* dirge for the living. And all these sounds repeated themselves, as if some mad god were howling from distant mountains.

Somewhere in my head a poem began. One of the lines was about those ducks, the loneliness and defeat the birds signified: "I think to the other side of that sound": I think to a place where uncertainty and loneliness are ended, to a happier time. But, I say to myself now, think again: I was never really happier than when I was lying in a sleeping bag on an Arctic island, listening to those noisy ducks at the top of the world and writing a poem. ("To See the Shore: A Preface," *The Collected Poems of Al Purdy*, p. xvi [1986])

Poetry. What is it for, what does it do, what is the use of it? In Canada, poetry reflects and foreshadows both country and people. It is the voice of reason, the voice of humanity, the voice that says "I am me." It allows us to know each other; like the CBC, it connects with all parts of the country. It says the little village of Ameliasburgh in Ontario has some relevance to, say, Granville Ferry in Nova Scotia. Above all, poetry says you are us and we are citizens of here and now, this space, this air, and this time. ("Disconnections," *Essays on Canadian Writing*, No. 49 [Summer 1993], p. 187)

I started to write at age twelve or thirteen, partly through interest in other people's writing (Bliss Carman, Robert Louis Stevenson, G.K.Chesterton, for example), but probably the largest reason was my own ego. I wanted attention. I think that is the principal reason for many youthful activities. ("Disconnections," *Essays on Canadian Writing*, No. 49 [Summer 1993], p. 213)

One question about poems has always puzzled me: why do I write them? At first the reason was sheer ego, I wanted attention . . . . But that original reason for writing has been succeeded by others, among them a raging desire for some kind of personal excellence, whose validity would endure against time. And yet that is a paradox, since I think a poem's validity belongs, principally, to its own particular moment of creation. Therefore, all are a series of moments emerging from their own time. At least they emerge as their own kind of truth, if the impulses that created them were valid in the first place. (*A Handful of Earth*, p. [8] [1977])

As a writer, I've always felt like an eternal amateur. Even after writing poems all my life, I'm never entirely confident that the next poem will find its way into being. And then I find myself writing one, without knowing exactly how I got there. ("To See the Shore: A Preface," *The Collected Poems of Al Purdy*, p. xviii [1986])

To my mind, what a poem ought to do is cause the reader to feel and think, balanced on nearly the same moment as myself when I wrote it. And I'd prefer to be understood with a minimum of mental strain by people as intelligent or more so than myself. I'd like them to hear the poem aloud when they read it on the page, which some people can do with poems they like.

Ideally, I'd like to say a thing so well that if the reader encounters a passage in a poem of mine which has much the same rhythm and ordinariness as this prose passage he or she is reading now: that that passage would suddenly glow like coloured glass in a black and white world. Which is probably a hopeless ambition. (*Bursting into Song*, p. 11 [1982])

[Poems] are my umbilical cord with the world and with other people, a two-way cord. They connect with sources I'm not even aware of, and if I were the poems would be impossible. What was it Yeats said about poems being "a quarrel with one's self"? Probably true, with inner arguments resolved or not in poems. (*A Handful of Earth*, p. [8] [1977])

[In my love poems] it isn't just the euphoric dreams of lovers I want to evoke, it's the ridiculosity inherent in the whole comic disease. And the mordant happiness of despair as well. Pain and its red blot in the brain, sorrow that things end, fade into little rags of memory that haunt us in their absence. (How wonderful to be made of stone and endure forever! Except, in some mysterious way, that which has existed truly once does last forever.) ("On Being Romantic," *Love in a Burning Building*, p. [10] [1970])

Well, what does the reader want from a poem? . . . Primarily, I suppose, to be entertained. And that involves tuning in on some emotion or feeling or discovery that is larger and more permanent than he is. Some flashing insight that adds a new perspective to living. Values also. And that is a great deal. Most of the time it's asking far too much. ("Leonard Çohen: A Personal Look," *Starting from Ameliasburgh*, p. 197 [1965, 1995])

Re intent, I prefer Earle Birney's opinion . . . that whatever meaning or levels of meaning the reader "extracts" from the work, this meaning is legitimate and valid. Because (my own comment as well as Birney's) there is something in a writer's head which causes him or her to incorporate meanings and possible interpretations he (or she) doesn't even know are there. ("Margaret Atwood's *The Journals of Susanna Moodie*," *Starting from Ameliasburgh*, pp. 239–40 [1971, 1995])

Rhyme and metre are not outdated, and I'm sure Pound must have suspected that. Both have lasted a thousand years, and will last many more . . . . I quite often use rhyme myself, and metre as well, trying to vary and conceal it within poems where it isn't expected and seems accidental if you do notice it. But I generally let a poem go where it seems to want to go, then touch it here and there deliberately, add metre say, or remove metre, add or remove a rhyme if too close to another rhyme. Perhaps it's not quite as artless as you seem to think? (Letter to George Johnston, 10 Aug. 1980)

Your mention of the "circular route" is also appropriate, since many poems I write are circular, that is coming back to some remark at the beginning in order to — not become self-contained — do what? I don't always know without looking at a particular poem: perhaps because our own lives seem to me circular in many ways, in that we never escape our own past and are always affected by it, and a poem's past is our own in minuscule. (Letter to George Galt, 25 Dec. 1978)

I dislike the strong implication that to employ natural speech idioms is the best or only way to write poetry. There seem to me to be a million ways to write a poem. To exclude any of them is to make academic strictures on what poems are and should be. ("Charles Bukowski's *It Catches My Heart in its Hands*," *Starting from Ameliasburgh*, p. 190 [1964, 1995])

I snapped out of that lost soul condition in the air force during the war years; and found new prosodic mentors in Vancouver in 1950. Dylan Thomas, of course, was the foremost of these.

I learned much from Layton in Montreal during my stint there in 1956 and later. And then I think I was overwhelmed by my own discoveries of new writers. It was wonderful to roll and tumble in the loose and magnificent rhythms of Yeats, the stern and sometimes puzzling disciplines of Auden, and most of all to be fascinated and enthralled by Lawrence. I don't say Lawrence is the best of those three, but he's the writer I learned most from, and whose own life was equally fascinating to me. (*Reaching for the Beaufort Sea*, pp. 286–7 [1993])

Lawrence learned much from Walt Whitman, and I can see how and why he could do so. Yet Whitman's work seems to me nearly mindless cliché by comparison to Lawrence's, despite Randall Jarrell's panegyric. (I want to like a poet because of his or her effect on me now, not for past influence on poetry in general.) Lawrence was drawn by Whitman's tone, his openness of line, his running on and on wherever thought would take him. Whitman refused to be dictated to by other men's thinking, by traditions of prosody, by the pretentious notion that if one was writing a poem one must say what a poem was supposed to say, must scan and rhyme.

Lawrence knew that a poem could say anything. The *I*s and *T*s could dance together on paper, the *A*s and *L*s could fly to the moon without wings. Words anchored his thought to paper so that the mind became corporeal and yet weightless. So that he wrote his life in his poems, and toward the end of his life he wrote his death. When a poet

— myself in this case — is influenced enough by Lawrence, then he escapes all influence, including Lawrence. After DHL, all other influences merge seamlessly into your own work. You learn still, you always learn, but never again are you under a slavish obligation to another writer. ("Disconnections," *Essays on Canadian Writing*, No. 49, [Summer 1993] p. 216.)

In my lifetime, there have been many other writers whose work I've admired and absorbed. They are constantly nudging me somewhere in my unconscious mind. If I had to name two of the most important influences, D.H.Lawrence and Irving Layton would qualify. As examples, not tutors. And perhaps Milton Acorn gets in there somewhere as well; I learned from him both how to write and how not to write. (Very few people can teach you opposite things at the same time.) I think I've learned from everyone I've read, on some level, though I've digested their writing in ways that make it impossible for me to recognize it in my own work. All of us who write are indebted to everyone else who writes for our enthusiasms and craft (or sullen art). ("To See the Shore: A Preface," *The Collected Poems of Al Purdy*, p. xviii [1986])

Northrop Frye's dictum that poems are created from poems seems to me partially true, in the sense that if other people's poems hadn't been written you couldn't have written your own. In that sense, what each of us writes balances and juggles the whole history of literature, and we are for that moment "the midland navel-stone" of earth. (*A Handful of Earth*, p. [8] [1977])

. . . you always choose and place poems [in a book] in such a way that they set each other off to advantage, opposites in mood or subject together or likes together. At least you hope they set each other off to advantage. (*Bursting into Song*, p. 10 [1982])

I read reviews to find out what's wrong with my writing; I read them for flattery and for truth, two opposite things. I regard myself as an odd kind of mainstream poet, and much closer to the style of mainstream American writers than British. And "mainstream" may be regarded here, in my case, as eccentric-conventional . . . . Paradoxically, while I write more like Canadian and US poets in style and diction, I like the slightly older British poets much better than the American ones. (*Reaching for the Beaufort Sea*, p. 283 [1993])

Travelling has almost been a way of life for this poet, especially in the last few years. Strange landscapes and foreign climes have produced a feeling of renewal, the earth itself has given me a sense of history, the stimulus of the original events carrying over in time and entering my own brain. ("To See the Shore: A Preface," *The Collected Poems of Al Purdy*, p. xv [1986])

And as a passing comment, there are few things I find more irritating about my own country than this so-called "search for an identity," an identity which I've never doubted having in the first place.

The environment, the land, the people, and the flux of history have made us what we are; these have existed since Canada's beginning, along with a capacity for slow evolvement into something else that goes on and on. And perhaps I would also include pride. Their total is all that any nation may possess. I think it is enough. ("Introduction," *The New Romans*, p. iii [1969])

Books by Al Purdy

POETRY:

The Enchanted Echo (1944)
Pressed on Sand (1955)
Emu, Remember! (1956)
The Crafte So Long to Lerne (1959)
The Blur in Between: Poems 1960–61 (1962)
Poems for All the Annettes (1962)
The Cariboo Horses (1965)
North of Summer: Poems from Baffin Island (1967)
Wild Grape Wine (1968)
Love in a Burning Building (1970)
The Quest for Ouzo (1971)
Hiroshima Poems (1972)
Selected Poems (1972)
On the Bearpaw Sea (1973)
Sex and Death (1973)
In Search of Owen Roblin (1974)
The Poems of Al Purdy: A New Canadian Library Selection (1976)
Sundance at Dusk (1976)
A Handful of Earth (1977)
At Marsport Drugstore (1977)
Moths in the Iron Curtain (1977)
No Second Spring (1977)
Being Alive: Poems 1958–78 (1978)
The Stone Bird (1981)
Birdwatching at the Equator: The Galapagos Islands (1982)
Bursting into Song: An Al Purdy Omnibus (1982)
Piling Blood (1984)
The Collected Poems of Al Purdy (1986)
The Woman on the Shore (1990)
Naked With Summer in Your Mouth (1994)

EDITOR:

The New Romans: Candid Canadian Opinions of the US (1968)
Fifteen Winds: A Selection of Modern Canadian Poems (1969)
Milton Acorn, *I've Tasted My Blood: Poems 1956–1968* (1969)

Storm Warning: The New Canadian Poets (1971)
Storm Warning 2: The New Canadian Poets (1976)
Andrew Suknaski, *Wood Mountain Poems* (1976)

OTHER:

No Other Country (prose, 1977)
The Bukowski / Purdy Letters 1964–1974: A Decade of Dialogue (with Charles Bukowski, 1983)
Morning and It's Summer: A Memoir (1983)
The George Woodcock–Al Purdy Letters (edited by George Galt, 1987)
A Splinter in the Heart (novel, 1990)
Cougar Hunter (essay on Roderick Haig-Brown, and letters between Haig-Brown and Purdy, 1993)
Margaret Laurence–Al Purdy: A Friendship in Letters (1993)
Reaching for the Beaufort Sea: An Autobiography (1993)
Starting from Ameliasburgh: The Collected Prose of Al Purdy (1995)